Comments on other *Amazing Stories* from readers & reviewers

*"Tightly written volumes filled with lots of wit and humour
about famous and infamous Canadians."*
Eric Shackleton, *The Globe and Mail*

*"The heightened sense of drama and intrigue, combined with a
good dose of human interest is what sets* Amazing Stories *apart."*
Pamela Klaffke, *Calgary Herald*

*"This is popular history as it should be... For this price,
buy two and give one to a friend."*
Terry Cook, a reader from Ottawa, on **Rebel Women**

*"Glasner creates the moment of the explosion itself in
graphic detail...she builds detail upon gruesome detail
to create a convincingly authentic picture."*
Peggy McKinnon, *The Sunday Herald*, on **The Halifax Explosion**

*"It was wonderful...I found I could not put it down.
I was sorry when it was completed."*
Dorothy F. from Manitoba on **Marie-Anne Lagimodière**

*"Stories are rich in description, and bristle
with a clever, stylish realness."*
Mark Weber, *Central Alberta Advisor*, on **Ghost Town Stories II**

*"A compelling read. Bertin...has selected only the most intriguing
tales, which she narrates with a wealth of detail."*
Joyce Glasner, *New Brunswick Reader*, on **Strange Events**

*"The resulting book is one readers will want to share
with all the women in their lives."*
Lynn Martel, *Rocky Mountain Outlook*, on **Women Explorers**

# D-DAY

# D-DAY

## Canadian Heroes of the Famous World War II Invasion

**HISTORY/MILITARY**

## by Tom Douglas

PUBLISHED BY ALTITUDE PUBLISHING CANADA LTD.
1500 Railway Avenue, Canmore, Alberta  T1W 1P6
www.altitudepublishing.com
1-800-957-6888

Publisher          Stephen Hutchings
Associate Publisher     Kara Turner
Editor          Jill Foran
Digital photo colouration and map     Scott Manktelow

We acknowledge the financial support of the Government
of Canada through the Book Publishing Industry Development
Program (BPIDP) for our publishing activities.

**Altitude GreenTree Program**
Altitude Publishing will plant twice as many trees as were used
in the manufacturing of this product.

**National Library of Canada Cataloguing in Publication Data**

CIP Data for this title is available on request from the Publisher.
Fax (403) 678-6951 for the attention of the Publishing Records Department.

ISBN 1-55153-795-8

An application for the trademark for Amazing Stories™
has been made and the registered trademark is pending.

Printed and bound in Canada by Friesens
2  4  6  8  9  7  5  3  1

Cover: "Nan White" beach, showing the 9th Canadian Infantry Brigade
landing on D-Day, June 6, 1944

To those who never came back, to those who did,
and to those who kept the home fires burning

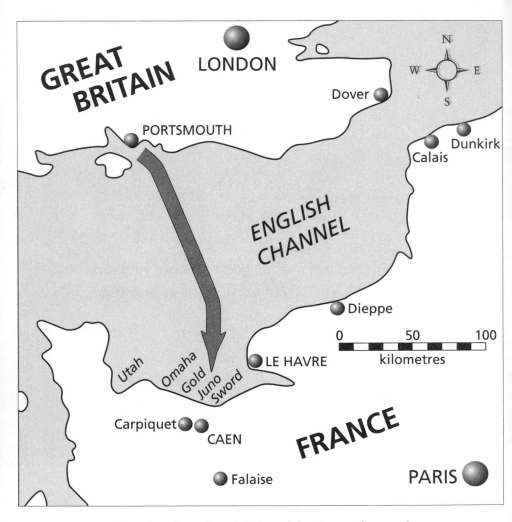

Map of southern Great Britain and the Normandy area of
France including D-Day landing beaches.

# Contents

# Prologue

*Sergeant Mel Douglas couldn't sleep. The adrenaline and the lot of rum had worn off, leaving him with a splitting headache and a queasy feeling in his gut. The violent lurching of the invasion craft only added to his misery, and he decided to see if he could get a breath of fresh air on deck.*

*As he reeled along the vessel's heaving corridor — two steps forward and one step back — he knew he'd never make it up on deck before his innards protested at the combination of army rations, overproof rum, and pre-battle hysteria rolling around in the pit of his stomach. He decided to make a brief stop in the latrine.*

*When he got there, he was taken aback by the sight of another soldier standing at one of the sinks. It was 0300, and the invasion was only hours away. Most of his comrades were sleeping fitfully wherever they had been able to find a convenient place to offload their gear and nod off before their call to arms.*

*"Moe, what the hell — excuse me — what the heck are you doing shaving when we're only hours away from hitting the beach?" the Canadian Army sergeant blurted.*

# D-Day

*He'd apologized for swearing because his fellow soldier, Sergeant Murray O. Kirby, was a religious man who'd been a Sunday school teacher back in his hometown of Oshawa, Ontario, before the war. Every Sunday during the 19th Field Regiment's pre-invasion stint in England, Murray had rounded up the hung-over members of his regiment and gently coerced them into attending an impromptu church service he held wherever he could find space — sometimes in an open field, sometimes an abandoned shed.*

*"Oh, hello Mel," Kirby said in his usual upbeat manner. "You couldn't sleep either, eh? I'm shaving because you never know when you're going to meet your Maker and I want to look my best."*

*"Don't talk like that, Moe," Douglas replied. "We're going to be okay. We have a rendezvous all worked out, remember? I'm buying you the best steak dinner the Windsor Hotel can come up with when you make it to Sault Ste. Marie. And you're going to reciprocate at the Genosh when I get to Oshawa. We have a deal."*

*"Sure Mel, we have a deal," the other man replied, his ear-to-ear grin dissolving into a wistful smile. He made one last swipe at the remaining lather on his chin, ran his razor under the tap, and splashed water on his face. "See you in the Soo, Mel."*

*Hours later, Sergeant Douglas was running a zigzag pattern up the carnage-strewn beach at St. Aubin-sur-Mer when he saw a half-track take a direct hit from a German mortar*

# Prologue

*just a few metres in front of him. Two of the occupants were killed instantly, and two others fell to the rocky beach where they were immediately attended to by medical personnel.*

*It wasn't until much later in the day, when the Canadians had established a beachhead on their D-Day objective, that Sergeant Mel Douglas learned one of the charred corpses he had seen sprawled grotesquely in the front seat of the half-track was his best buddy, Sergeant Murray O. Kirby.*

# *Chapter 1*
# War ... Again

The Great War — The War To End All Wars. That's what they'd called the senseless and tragic carnage of 1914–1918 that had turned Europe into a charnel house for at least 10 million bodies — nobody was ever able to calculate the exact magnitude of the slaughter. The number of Canadians who had "paid the supreme sacrifice" had been rounded off to a neat and tidy 66,000 by those whose job it was to come up with such statistics.

But the war to end all wars had proven to be not so great after all. It produced an uneasy peace for less than 21 years, from November 11, 1918, until September 1, 1939. On the latter date, Nazi Germany blitzkrieged its crack troops and tanks across the virtually defenceless Polish border while swarms of illegally manufactured Stukas and Messerschmitts strafed and carpet bombed the country's hapless inhabitants.

Nazi dictator Adolf Hitler — Der Führer or The Leader, as his enthralled followers lovingly called him — had flagrantly ignored the sanctions placed against Germany by the victorious and vindictive nations that had set down the terms of surrender in the Treaty of Versailles signed on June 28, 1919. Under the guise of turning out industrial machinery and a "people's car" — the Volkswagen — to help rebuild his impoverished country, Hitler had overseen the mass production of a deadly arsenal of weaponry and war materiel. The leaders of the Western nations, frantically hoping to avoid another war, had turned a blind eye to this and other infractions until the emboldened Nazi leader had taken the first step on the road of no return by invading Poland.

In retrospect, it's easy to understand why the people of Germany allowed this little Austrian corporal from World War I — the name now given to The Great War since the world was at war once again — to plunge them into another massive conflict. They had nothing to lose. The financial reparations the signers of the Versailles Peace Treaty had levelled against Germany — the "stab in the back" as Hitler disdainfully called it — had brought their defeated country to the brink of despair. While Germans used wheelbarrows to cart huge piles of inflation-ravaged Deutschmarks to the local bakery to buy bread for their starving children, their French neighbours swarmed over the border to gorge themselves on German pastries for a pittance in their currency.

Like a schoolboy repeatedly knocking a chip off the shoulder of a blustering bully, Hitler kept breaking Versailles embargo after Versailles embargo by reoccupying lands taken from Germany at the 1919 peace negotiations. A timid Western world, personified forever by the "peace in our time" naivety of British Prime Minister Neville Chamberlain, finally drew a line at the Polish border. Hitler crossed it.

World War II had begun.

### Canada Takes A Stand

Great Britain and France declared war on Germany on September 3, 1939. Traditionally, Canada would have been included automatically in that declaration as a British "colony." But a hill in Northern France had changed all that back in April 1917.

It took the blood of more than 10,000 Canadians, killed and wounded, to capture Hill 145 on a ridge near the French town of Arras in an assault that began on Easter Sunday of that long-ago April. When the attack was over, the Canadians had secured the entire Vimy Ridge, as well as a place in history as a gallant fighting force. Possibly for the first time, Canadians started regarding themselves as an independent nation, not just as a willing source of men and arms for the British war machine.

So when Great Britain and France declared themselves

at war with Nazi Germany, Canada didn't take a knee-jerk jump into the fray. As with everything in life, of course, there were extenuating circumstances. It wasn't just a case of a common belief that, as an independent nation, Canada should make up its own mind. The bonds of patriotism were still very solid, and war fever swept the land. But there was enough dissent to cause the Canadian government to hold back.

The country had been devastated by the Great Depression of the 1930s, and its capabilities in terms of trained troops and war machinery were laughable. Furthermore, only a brief generation had passed since so many young Canadian lives had been snuffed out or altered horribly on the killing fields of WWI. A number of Canadians felt that this time it was Europe's war and that Canada's role should be no more than that of being the Allies' breadbasket — supplying the warriors of Great Britain and France with Canadian wheat, beef, and other foodstuffs. Once the Depression-idled factories got up and running again, there would also be the possibility of sending over tanks, aircraft, and other military hardware. And the country was quite willing to allow the vast expanse of its skies to be used as an open-air classroom under the British Commonwealth Air Training Plan.

This semi-pacifist stance didn't last long, however. When the newsreels started popping up in local movie houses showing the ruthless might of the Nazi juggernaut as it rolled over Poland, patriotic fervour flared up and prompted the Canadian Parliament to declare war on Germany on September 10.

The prevailing sentiment remained that Canada would fight a limited war as a backup to the larger and better-equipped British and French forces. But Hitler had a few surprises up his swastika-emblazoned sleeve that would soon catapult Canada into the very midst of the battlefield.

**Talent For Showmanship**

Der Führer had played the "buffoon" card to great advantage time and again. He had a knack for lulling those who could have put a stop to him along the way into believing that he was all bluff and no substance. He had the rich and wealthy in his country convinced that his talents for showmanship and daring could be channelled into returning Germany to the world stage. They felt certain that he could be manipulated as a figurehead, a puppet who would dance to the tune of the industrialists who were supporting his National Socialist Party as a buffer against communism.

By the time the German Establishment realized that what they had in fact was a vicious tiger by the tail, Hitler and his henchmen had eliminated all opposition and had taken control of the German Parliament, the Reichstag. World domination was next on the agenda.

The British and French were as easily fooled as the German industrialists. Their officers were still locked into the archaic thinking of World War I, when battles were fought by the rules and the antagonists would treat each other as gentlemen who just happened to be on opposing sides. They'd take this upstart Adolf Hitler, a lowly corporal, and show him a thing or two. Why, the war would be over by Christmas!

The only rules understood by Adolf Hitler, who had changed his name from Schikelgruber in the early stages of building a personality cult, were the rules of winning at all costs. The noble Polish aristocracy met his tanks with cavalry charges. He flattened them. The people of Holland hoped to negotiate a peaceful settlement. He enslaved them. The French built a concrete bunker system called the Maginot Line they considered impregnable. He sent his lightning-swift assault troops around the end of it. The British and French prepared to make a gallant stand in Northern France in the spring of 1940. He drove them into the sea at Dunkirk.

Within a few short months of being sent to England to train with the British military, the raw and ill-equipped troops of the 1st Canadian Infantry Division found themselves, with the fall of France in June 1940, as the ranking ally of Great Britain. Russia had signed a non-aggression pact with the Nazis and their Axis partner Italy, and the United States was still in an isolationist mood, refusing to get involved. Popguns and paper darts were all that seemed to stand between freedom and Adolf Hitler's plans for world conquest.

# D-Day

## Hitler's Lightning War Sputters

The luck of the draw. It's a factor that has turned the tide of battle from time immemorial. Military historians still turn apoplectic over their port wine and Stilton cheese as they argue the "what ifs" of campaigns waged by generals from Pompey to Patton. "What if Henry V hadn't been blessed with archers using the deadly longbow at the Battle of Agincourt?" they ruminate. "What if Napoleon hadn't been suffering from a bout of haemorrhoids at Waterloo?"

In Britain's — and Canada's — lonely stance against Hitler's hordes, the luck of the draw entered into the equation on a number of occasions, several of which were particularly decisive.

In the first place, no one, least of all Hitler and his Luftwaffe chief Hermann Göring, could have predicted the tenacity and courage of the Royal Air Force, whose members would receive high praise from Winston Churchill when he said of them: "Never in the field of human conflict was so much owed by so many to so few." British pilots, backed up by volunteer airmen from Canada and refugee fliers from some of the Nazi-conquered countries, fought Göring's German air force to a standstill during the Battle of Britain from July to October 1940.

More than 100 Canadian pilots took part in this epic battle, some in the all-Canadian Royal Air Force (RAF) 242 Squadron, and the remainder with various British squadrons. Twenty Canadians lost their lives in the day-after-day skirmishes with the Luftwaffe. On August 30, No. 242 Squadron attacked a formation of more than 100 German aircraft and shot down a dozen or more, without any losses to the squadron.

No. 1 Squadron Royal Canadian Air Force (RCAF) was the first intact Canadian fighter pilot unit to arrive in Britain, crossing the Atlantic in ships, with Canadian-built Hawker Hurricanes accompanying them in wooden crates. Arriving during the height of the Battle of Britain, they learned their operational training between skirmishes. Later renamed No. 401, the squadron became the first RCAF unit to tackle the Luftwaffe, shooting down three German bombers and damaging four others over southern England. The Canadians lost only one Hurricane.

By the time the Battle of Britain was over in mid-October, No. 1 Squadron had shot down 31 German aircraft, with another 43 "probables." The Canadian losses were 16 Hurricanes and three pilots. Flight Lieutenant Gordon R. McGregor was credited with five "kills" and awarded the Distinguished Flying Cross (DFC).

The pilots' bravery and their refusal to give up was matched by the incredible will of the people of Great Britain who carried on regardless during the Luftwaffe raids that left the cities of London and Coventry in shambles after many nights of intense bombing.

A lucky break for the beleaguered Brits was Hitler's mad decision to emulate Napoleon's folly by invading Russia, launching Operation Barbarossa in June 1941. That move brought a powerful ally, the Soviet Union, into the anti-German camp.

Then came Japan's raid on Pearl Harbor on December 7, 1941 — U.S. President Franklin Roosevelt's "day of infamy" that saw the military might of the U.S. join the Allied cause against the German/Italian/Japanese Axis partnership. British civilians who watched the American troops' friendly "invasion" of their cities, towns, and villages would complain that there were only four things wrong with those Yanks: "They're overfed, overpaid, oversexed and over here!" But American wealth, industrial strength, and sheer manpower would turn the tide that would eventually lead to a total Allied victory a few years hence.

**Raid on St-Nazaire**
A British commando raid on a small French port was the tip of the spear that led to one of the worst disasters in Canadian military history. The British Army, despite — or perhaps in retaliation for — its ignominious retreat from Dunkirk in the spring of 1940, carried out a series of commando raids on French ports over the next several years, even though their successes were spotty at best and the raids resulted in numerous British casualties.

On March 28, 1942, Operation Chariot was launched against the heavily fortified Atlantic port of St-Nazaire. The objective was to destroy the *Normandie* dock, the only repair site on the Atlantic coast large enough to handle the newest German battleship, the *Tirpitz*. If the dock were destroyed, it would prevent the battleship from being serviced between its raids on Allied convoys — naval-escorted merchant ships bringing vital war supplies from North America.

The St-Nazaire raid, comprised of some 600 British commandos in wooden motor launches and the destroyer *Campbelltown* (whose orders were to ram the dock gate), took the Germans by surprise. The commandos made it into the harbour before experiencing any enemy fire. They destroyed dock machinery and set depth charges at crucial points around the dry dock.

The German troops occupying the port eventually regained control, and most of the commandos were either killed or captured, with a few managing to escape by boat or on foot into the French countryside. While the Germans were interrogating their prisoners and inspecting the crippled *Campbelltown*, tons of explosives hidden in the destroyer's forward holds blew sky-high. The dry dock was so badly damaged it would not be repaired until after the war. The battleship *Tirpitz* never did see action in the Atlantic and eventually was sunk by British bombers.

The British Combined Operations planners were thrilled with this "victory," in spite of the loss of close to 600 crack troops. In war, after all, soldiers are expendable — especially to those military strategists who sleep between clean sheets in commandeered mansions, far from the theatre of war.

And the real tragedy was yet to come. The "successful" raid on St-Nazaire left Combined Operations with the mistaken impression that it was quite all right to attack heavily fortified ports by direct assault if the defenders were taken by surprise. By the time they discovered the stupidity of that assumption, many hundreds of Canadian troops would lie dead on the beaches of a little resort town called Dieppe.

# Chapter 2
# Dry Run Or
# Strategic Blunder?

The battle cry "Don't worry, men, it'll be a piece of cake!" hasn't exactly gone down in the annals of World War II heroic phrases with the likes of Churchill's, "We shall fight them on the beaches" or General Douglas MacArthur's, "I shall return!" And for good reason. It was blurted out by Major General J. Hamilton "Ham" Roberts, commander of the 2nd Canadian Infantry Division. His audience consisted of some 4961 infantry soldiers and tank crews, 1075 British commandos, 50 U.S. Army Rangers, 15 Free French soldiers, and 5 expatriate German interpreters preparing to embark on what a number of war historians still believe was a suicide mission.

By the spring of 1942, Soviet leader Joseph Stalin was

clamouring for a Second Front — an Allied invasion of Nazi-held Europe that would divert some of Hitler's military forces from Russia, taking the pressure off that beleaguered nation. Stalin's demand set the stage for a chain of events that would send Canadian troops into battle like lambs to the slaughter. Most of them were in their late teens or early twenties. Some, who had lied about their age, were still too young to shave.

Part of the blame rests with Canadian politicians, Canadian military planners, and, perversely, even the lowly Canadian soldiers languishing in England, where they'd been stationed on training manoeuvres for more than two years. The Canadian politicians sought a positive turn of events that would help them get re-elected. The military planners sought glory that would turn their post-war memoirs into best-sellers. The soldiers sought relief from the boredom of running up and down sand dunes playing war games on the south coast of England.

When the raid on St-Nazaire persuaded Allied High Command that a direct assault could be made safely on a fortified port, the military planners began casting around for an operation that would satisfy the American-supported Russian demand for the opening of a Second Front. It was also apparently the British view that before a full-scale invasion of Europe could be launched, a preliminary probe was needed to sound out the enemy's strengths and weaknesses. And it would test the Allied troops' abilities to launch a seaborne offensive.

*Dry Run Or Strategic Blunder?*

The French seaside port of Dieppe, about halfway between Calais and Le Havre on the Channel coast, was eventually chosen as the target for a raid in early July. There were several reasons for the selection of this target. It was near enough to the launch areas of southern England to be reached by ship under cover of darkness. It was well within the operating range of Allied fighter planes that could provide air cover without running low on fuel. And it was heavily enough fortified that the Allies felt they could learn a great deal about German defence tactics before the launch of a major assault.

**Not Since Gallipoli**
Military strategists were rubbing their hands gleefully over the opportunity to see how Allied troops fared in handling an assault fleet off an enemy coast. The last major amphibious landing, after all, had been at Gallipoli in World War I. As a bonus, there would be an opportunity to test out new types of assault craft and equipment, and Allied officers would gain hands-on experience in capturing and holding an enemy port.

The Dieppe raid would have the additional practical benefits of destroying German defences, dock and rail installations, gasoline dumps, and radar stations — not to mention the capture of German prisoners and military documents.

In their determination to get some action going, Combined Ops disregarded British intelligence estimates of the strength of the Dieppe defences. They dismissed the local German garrison as being made up of raw recruits, older men not fit for combat duty, and Polish conscripts who had failed the tests for joining their own army in 1939.

The planners also turned a blind eye to the fact that the town beach was flanked by two high headlands, and that beyond these were unassailable chalk cliffs strengthened by concrete artillery pillboxes, anti-aircraft batteries, and machine-gun nests.

Some skeptics insist to this day that the Allies were looking for cannon fodder to convince the Russians and Americans that a cross-Channel assault was not feasible, at least not so soon. However, in honour of those who died on the Dieppe beaches, the preferred scenarios are that at worst it was a tragic Allied blunder, and at best it was an essential exercise that taught many valuable lessons, making the eventual invasion of Europe the overwhelming success that it was.

At any rate, the story goes that when Lieutenant-General Bernard Montgomery, then chief of Britain's Southeast Command, asked Canada's senior officer in Britain, Lieutenant-General A.G.L. McNaughton, whether the Canadians wanted the job, McNaughton replied, "You bet we want it." He would suggest after the war: "The responsibility was mine and nobody else's. The final decision was mine. I said yes. And I say quite frankly that if I were in exactly the same position I would do exactly the same thing tomorrow."

## Operation Jubilee

They called the exercise "Operation Jubilee" — the latter word described in the Oxford Reference Dictionary as a time of rejoicing. It was anything but.

The Canadian attack force included The Essex Scottish from Windsor, Ontario; The Royal Regiment from Toronto; The Royal Hamilton Light Infantry; The Cameron Highlanders of Winnipeg, Manitoba; The South Saskatchewan Regiment; and Les Fusiliers Mont-Royal. The Calgary Tank Regiment sported new 6-pounder guns on their 40-ton Churchill tanks, and detachments of Montreal's Black Watch and Régiment de Maisonneuve, as well as The Calgary Highlanders and Toronto Scottish, were at the ready.

The assault, which was to be launched at 0450 hours on August 19,1942, was probably the worst-kept secret of World War II. It had been postponed five times in early July due to bad weather — with the troops clambering on and off the attack vessels like daytrippers to Toronto's Centre Island, and complaining bitterly about it to anyone within earshot.

When it was suggested to Chief of Combined Operations Lord Louis Mountbatten that this breach of security should mean the end of Dieppe as the target, he obtusely replied that the Germans surely would not expect another planned assault on the same place after word had leaked out about the earlier aborted attacks. It was a gross error in judgement that Canadians would pay for dearly with their lives.

And so, despite the misgivings of many, the final planning took place for the Dieppe raid. After the war, the deputy commander of the operation, Brigadier Churchill Mann, outlined the details of how things were supposed to have gone:

"H-Hour was 4:50 a.m. Because of lack of sea room and of trained landing craft crews, the four flank attacks (Yellow, Blue, Green and Orange beaches) had to be launched half an hour ahead of the frontal attack across the main Dieppe beaches (Red and White).

"On the far left, British commandos were to destroy the gun battery at Berneval. Landing at Puys, The Royal Regiment and a company of The Black Watch were to destroy guns on the east headland overlooking Dieppe harbour.

"On the extreme right, commandos were to destroy the Varengeville battery. At Pourville, The South Saskatchewan Regiment was to land astride the River Scie. Thirty minutes later, The Cameron Highlanders would advance through the Saskatchewans' beachhead, move inland, join tanks from Dieppe and assault an airdrome and a German divisional headquarters believed to be at Arques.

"There were to be two other attacks at H-hour plus 30 minutes. On the left half of the beach at Dieppe, The Essex Scottish and tanks of The Calgary Regiment were to land simultaneously and advance rapidly into the town to secure the harbour area for engineer demolition. On the right half of the Dieppe beach, the RHLI (Royal Hamilton Light Infantry) would land with other Calgary tanks and move through the town to secure exits for other tanks to proceed inland where they would join the Camerons.

"Les Fusiliers Mont-Royal were to land later, occupying the perimeter of the town after the Essex and RHLI had seized it. All Canadian units were to withdraw across the main Dieppe beaches, with the FMR serving as rearguard.

"The British commandos on the extreme left and right flanks would withdraw from the beaches on which they had landed."

It looked good on paper.

On the evening of August 18, a naval force consisting of seven Royal Navy destroyers, one Polish destroyer, and a number of smaller war craft manned by Britons, Canadians, and a few Free French, set out from England to carry out the raid across the Channel.

At first, everything went according to plan. The fleet passed effortlessly through the German amphibian minefield that had been cleared hours earlier by 15 British minesweepers. Radio silence had been maintained, and no enemy ships or aircraft had been spotted. The critical element of surprise seemed to be holding. About 20 kilometres off the French coast, the crews began preparing the landing craft, and the tedious operation of getting the assault troops into these small boats was accomplished without a hitch.

**Disaster Strikes**

At that point, however, everything began to go wrong. At

0347 hours — 63 minutes before H-Hour — 23 landing craft and their three escorts ran into a small German coastal convoy of five cargo ships and three armed escorts steaming for Dieppe. It was later learned that the convoy had been spotted twice on British radar the night before and two warnings had been sent to the assault force. However, due to "technical difficulties" aboard the command ship, the destroyer HMS *Calpe*, neither message was received.

Before the Allied assault troops could take evasive action, a star shell illuminated the night sky, and the jig was up. The Germans opened fire, and the Allied landing craft — unarmed and unarmoured — sped off in all directions. The British gunboats escorting the landing craft returned the fire, and at least two German ships were sunk.

But the crucial element of surprise was lost, and German shore batteries began opening fire on the incoming landing craft. By the time the troops were able to get free of the vessels and begin wading ashore, the entire German garrison was ready for them — mowing down wave after wave with machine-gun fire, mortars, and everything else at hand.

What made things worse was that no preliminary aerial bombing had softened up the Germans' defences, and there was only brief naval shelling. This tactical blunder was partly due to the planners' concern for the safety of the townspeople, and partly because of their fears that the resulting rubble would make the streets impassable to tanks. In addition, the Royal Navy (RN) had insisted it couldn't spare a battleship and the RAF had declined to contribute any bombers.

The only firepower the assault troops could pin their hopes on were the Churchill tanks, but their treads could not negotiate the baseball-sized pebbles on the beach and they soon bogged down to become sitting ducks for the German guns.

In addition, German snipers on the cliffs identified Allied officers and signalmen, putting bullets through their heads and their radios, thereby depriving the assault troops of both leadership and communications.

## Deadly Fire

Like shooting fish in a barrel, German machine gunners swept the beaches with deadly fire until their gun barrels were almost red-hot. German soldiers on the cliffs dropped stick grenades on the exposed Allied troops who had taken meagre shelter behind the shallow sea wall.

Whenever the story of the Dieppe Raid is told, the courage of the doomed invaders is proudly recounted by the survivors. One such tale involves Lieutenant Colonel Charles Merritt of Vancouver, B.C., who was with The South Saskatchewan Regiment on that day. Lieutenant Colonel Merritt led at least four groups of men across a bridge at Pourville swept by machine-gun, mortar, and artillery fire. Wounded twice, he personally destroyed a German pillbox by getting close enough to toss a grenade through its observation slit.

Lieutenant Colonel Merritt then stalked a sniper with a Bren gun and silenced him. As his troops retreated, he was last seen collecting weapons to hold off and "get even with" the enemy. He spent the rest of the war in a German prison camp. He was awarded the Commonwealth's highest honour, the Victoria Cross, for his acts of heroism.

Another hero was Commander (later Rear Admiral) Romuald Nalecz-Tyminski of Szenderow, Poland, who, as part of the British-based Polish Flotilla, disobeyed orders to keep his destroyer far enough offshore to avoid shelling by German batteries. Instead, he brought his ship within range time and again, eventually rescuing more than 80 Canadians trapped on the beach.

Joe Ryan, a veteran of The Royal Regiment of Canada, told the *Toronto Star*: "Nobody did more than [Nalecz-Tyminski] did to get the Canadians out." Ryan added that Commander Nalecz-Tyminski manoeuvred his destroyer, the *Slazak*, precariously close to shore with guns blazing in order to save the soldiers before turning abruptly, churning up mud and rocks from beneath the water. He was later award-ed the Distinguished Service Cross for his valiant efforts.

By 0700 hours, the outcome of the raid was tragically clear. By 0900 hours, those Allied troops who were still alive and mobile had surrendered. The results were horrendous. Of the close to 5000 Canadians who had formed the assault force, 907 were killed in action and 1946 were taken prisoner.

One of those prisoners, Sergeant-Major Lucien Dumais

of Les Fusiliers Mont-Royal, would escape from a cattle car
that was taking him and his fellow captives to a German concentration camp. He would make his way down through
France and across the Pyrenees Mountains to freedom —
only to agree to go back into Occupied France to set up an
escape network for Allied aircrew, escaped prisoners, and
agents on the run.

But for most of the Dieppe assault force, their story had
anything but a happy ending. The only consolation they or
their next of kin could take from the tragedy was that many
valuable lessons were learned that would save thousands of
Allied lives when the next — and final — cross-Channel
attack on Hitler's "Fortress Europe" took place less than two
years later.

# Chapter 3
# Preparing For Overlord

hile a number of other reversals would be suffered by the Allies before the war was won, Dieppe actually marked a turning point in the conflict that up until then had seen Germany making terrifying advances.

In November of 1942, the British trounced General Erwin Rommel's Afrika Korps at the Battle of El Alamein — for which General Bernard Montgomery was promoted and knighted. By May of 1943, the Germans had been kicked out of North Africa. The following month, the Battle of Stalingrad saw the Wehrmacht's 6th Army annihilated by the sheer might and tenacity of the Red Army. And in July, the 1st Canadian Infantry Division and a Canadian tank brigade joined other Allies in the invasion of Sicily. They would slug it out with the Italians and Germans for almost a year, with Rome being liberated on June 4, 1944 by a special force of tough Canadians and Americans the Germans nicknamed "The Devil's Brigade."

But even these victories couldn't erase the painful blow, both physical and mental, that the Canadians had suffered on August 19, 1942. From the standpoint of human carnage, Dieppe was a tragic event — undoubtedly the worst in Canadian military history. While higher numbers of Canadian casualties have resulted from other battles before and since, in terms of percentages of troops lost and objectives unachieved, Dieppe stands alone. It had been folly bordering on the insane to send troops into a heavily fortified port when vital security had almost certainly been breached and the equally vital need for pre-raid bombardment had all but been ignored.

Yet even the harshest critics of this abortive exercise have to acknowledge that it did teach the Allies a number of lessons for their next cross-Channel assault — Operation Overlord, the code name for the Normandy Invasion.

Almost as soon as the last stragglers who survived the Dieppe fiasco were back in England, military strategists began a post mortem to find out what went wrong and what would be needed to make things right the next time. They ruled out a raid on a heavily fortified port. They reconfirmed the need for absolute secrecy. They judged it essential that enemy defences be heavily bombed and shelled before the attack. It was determined that special equipment would be required to handle natural and German-laid obstacles on the landing beaches. And there was no doubt that massive numbers in terms of assault troops and materiel would be required to win the day.

### Largest Armada Ever

Thus began the build-up of the largest armada ever assembled in the history of warfare. It has been marvelled that Southern England didn't sink under the weight of so many Allied troops, military vehicles, and supplies.

Invasion plans called for 175,000 men, 1500 tanks, 10,000 other vehicles, and 3000 pieces of artillery to be transported across the Channel within the first 24 hours of the attack. Huge numbers of transport aircraft, troop-carrying gliders, and a vast array of invasion ships — destroyers, corvettes, frigates, and torpedo boats — would be required, as well as thousands of landing craft that would speed the troops to the beaches from the mother ships.

The shortage of landing craft at the time was given as one reason for the original invasion date of May 1, 1944, being put off for more than a month. Despite the efforts of American and British factories to turn out as many of these small assault vessels as possible, there was still a sizeable shortage as the crucial date approached. D-Day (even though there are fanciful explanations to the contrary, the "D" just

Operation Overlord assembled the largest-ever armada
of ships to cross the English Channel.

refers to the actual day of an attack) was postponed until May
31. Then it was discovered that an American general had
been hoarding landing craft for the eventual final push
against the Japanese in the Pacific theatre of war. He was
ordered to get the boats to England as quickly as possible.

Along with transportation vehicles, the British south
coast was soon jammed with vast numbers of tanks, half-
tracks, self-propelled and towed artillery, trucks, jeeps, and
every other kind of military vehicle deemed necessary for a
successful operation.

To avoid another tragedy, planners called for special equipment to handle beach landings. Some of it already existed, and some had to be invented based on the difficulties experienced in the Dieppe raid. There were floating artillery and rocket batteries, and a wide variety of modified tanks. There were amphibious tanks, bulldozer tanks to clear beach obstacles, flail tanks to beat through mine fields, Bobbins that laid rolls of artificial trackway across beach shingles for following tanks, Crocodiles that mounted large flamethrowers rather than guns, and AVREs (armoured vehicle royal engineers) that fired massive demolition mortars. Some of this new equipment had been tested during the landing in Sicily. Also stockpiled were huge stacks of weapons, fuel, munitions, equipment, and consumables for the assault troops.

Given all these preparations, it seems incredible that the surprise of the attack could be maintained. It came down to an approach that in later years would be known as hiding in plain sight. That the Allies would invade Europe was known to one and all, including the German High Command. Enemy reconnaissance planes, Nazi collaborators, and German spies working in England were filing reports about troop and materiel build-up.

The Allies took whatever precautions they could by hiding the materiel in wooded areas, under the trees of old lanes, in the shade of country mansions, in abandoned quarries, in rock caves, and under camouflage nets. Still, this was like trying to conceal a circus troupe under a pup tent. Rather than attempting to do the impossible, it was decided that as long as the enemy didn't know when or where the invasion troops would land, it wasn't all that important that they were aware of the build-up of men and materiel.

## A Tangled Web

As Winston Churchill said in 1943: "In wartime, truth is so precious that she must always be attended by a bodyguard of lies." The Allies thus embarked on an unprecedented campaign of deception that would keep the German High Command, and especially Adolf Hitler, unsure as to the timing and location of the invasion. The most logical attack area was the Pas de Calais, a mere 30 kilometres across the English Channel from Dover. It was essential that the Allies keep the Germans convinced right down to the last possible moment — and even beyond — that this was where the main assault force would land.

They did this through an incredible web of deceit. This involved feeding false information to known informants and broadcasting false radio reports that would be picked up by German eavesdroppers, including fake air traffic reports about activities in and around Dover as though that area's white cliffs would bear silent witness to the launch of the Allied armada.

The Allied troops in England training for the Invasion were subjected to rules of strict secrecy. Every letter was heavily censored and the men were ordered not to mention any place names. One young Canadian, in composing a letter home, wrote: "Dear Mother: Here I am in the place that I came to after I left the place that I was before. Before I left the place where I was before and came to the place I came to, I was at _(CENSORED)___."

To really keep the Germans off guard, there was even a scenario where the Allies leaked false information pointing to an invasion of Norway, with Sweden expected to join the war on the Allies' side, and a subsequent invasion of Germany coming through Denmark.

For every bomb that was dropped in the Normandy area to soften up German troop concentrations, railway lines, factories, and fortifications, another bomb was dropped in the Pas de Calais area. While troops and materiel were being assembled in the English ports across from the Normandy beaches, men and equipment that wouldn't be needed until later in the campaign were stationed at Dover under a fictitious army group headed by General George S. Patton. The Allies even manufactured plywood and canvas installations, as well as inflatable lifelike tanks, trucks, and other equipment, which they interspersed amongst the real thing to beef up the supposed attack forces for a Pas de Calais offensive.

Another major advantage the Allies had going for them was the fact that British cipher experts had managed to crack the German Enigma code. This remarkable breakthrough allowed Allied military strategists to tap in on Nazi secret electronic transmissions to make sure the deception was being swallowed by the German High Command.

The Germans were convinced that the Enigma output could not be broken, so they used this intricately coded machine for all sorts of communications — on the battle-field, at sea, in the sky, and, significantly, within their secret services. The British described any intelligence gained from Enigma as "Ultra," and considered it top secret.

### The Invasion Plan

Operation Overload called for the landing of five infantry divisions on an 80-kilometre expanse of the French coastline stretching between St. Germain-de-Varreville in the west to Rainville in the east. To those with just a passing knowledge of Northern France, the area, known as the Bay of Seine, is shaped like a bowl, with Cherbourg as the western lip, Le Havre as the eastern rim, and the invasion beaches forming the vessel's flat bottom.

The British Second Army — which included units of General H.D.G. Crerar's First Canadian Army — was given the task of forming the eastern side of the assault on three expanses of beach code-named Sword, Juno, and Gold. The First U.S. Army would invade two coastal sections code-named Omaha and Utah to the western side of the target. The 1st Canadian Parachute Battalion was ordered to precede the invasion force by jumping with the British 6th Airborne into the area behind the British and Canadian attack zones. Two

American divisions — the 82nd and 101st U.S. Airborne — would precede their U.S. colleagues to the west. Their objectives were to delay enemy movement of reinforcements into the vicinity, confuse the Germans as to the exact location and direction of the attack, and help the advancing Allied troops expand their beachhead.

The invasion planners designated the 3rd Canadian Infantry Division, under Major General R.F.L. Keller, as well as the 2nd Canadian Armoured Brigade, as the assault force. Two of the 3rd Division's three brigades would be the first wave to land at Juno Beach, which had been subdivided on the battle maps into two sectors that some planner decided to call Mike and Nan.

The Regina Rifle Regiment and The Royal Winnipeg Rifles of the 7th Infantry Brigade, as well as an attached company of The Canadian Scottish Regiment, would be the first to hit Mike sector. The rest of The Canadian Scottish would be held in reserve. First onto Nan sector would be the 8th Brigade's Queen's Own Rifles of Canada and The North Shore (New Brunswick) Regiment, backed up by Le Régiment de la Chaudière.

Buoyed by the new Direct Drive (DD) amphibious canvas flotation gear, the tanks of the 1st Hussars and The Fort Garry Horse would hit the beaches ahead of the infantry to blast away at German defences and provide covering fire. Guns of The Royal Canadian Artillery would commence firing from landing craft while still out in the Channel, and would then be swiftly put ashore to add support to the infantry and armour.

Support troops were slotted in for the attack. Sappers of the Royal Canadian Engineers would blast a path through any enemy obstacles not taken care of by the first wave of tanks. The Royal Canadian Corps of Signals would establish lines of communication. And The Royal Canadian Medical Corps, which later in the campaign included nursing sisters of No. 10 Canadian General Hospital, would attend to the wounded. The Royal Canadian Army Service Corps would be charged with the enormous task of seeing that the entire Canadian contingent was well supplied with food, fuel, ammunition, and other war materiel.

### Lessons From Dieppe

Students of military history might well ask how all these massive shipments of supplies could be offloaded in an area that made its livelihood from tourism rather than from serving as port terminals for incoming cargo. The Allies — still smarting from the fact that Dieppe, a harbour town, had been heavily fortified to protect its port facilities — had purposely selected the Normandy resort area because its defences were much lighter. Their rationale was that intelligence reports indicated the Germans had convinced themselves that the Allies would have to capture a port in order to deliver supplies. Since nothing in the Normandy area offered such facilities, it couldn't be the invasion point.

# D-Day

The Allied answer to this lack of port facilities was an ingenious plan to construct what they called Mulberry Harbours, first designed years before by Winston Churchill. These were gigantic concrete caissons — watertight chambers — that could be towed from England to France and sunk along with derelict ships off the invasion coast. The resultant breakwater would serve as a framework to which prefabricated piers could be attached to allow supply ships to unload their cargo directly onto transport vehicles.

The rest of the invasion plan for Juno Beach called for the Canadian units to make a successful landing on the beaches and capture the three small towns just behind the landing area: Courseulle-sur-Mer, Bernière-sur-Mer, and St-Aubin-sur-Mer. They would then advance some 15 kilometres inland to seize and hold the high ground west of the city of Caen, including the airfield at the nearby small town of Carpiquet, by the end of the first day. In anticipation of a Nazi counterattack, the successful invasion troops would be reinforced by the 9th Infantry Brigade — The Highland Light Infantry of Canada from Galt, Ontario, The Stormont, Dundas and Glengarry Highlanders, and The North Nova Scotia Highlanders — as well as the tanks of The Sherbrooke Fusiliers.

Artillery, machine gun and mortar units, signals and medical corps personnel, and other components would accompany the troops in all sectors as support units. In total, some 15,000 Canadians would comprise the initial landing force on Juno Beach and inland toward Caen. The rest of the First Canadian Army — its headquarters under General Crerar — as well as the 2nd Canadian Infantry Division and the 4th Canadian Armoured Division would join their comrades over the next few weeks. They would fight side by side in a valiant effort to drive the Germans out of France and back through Belgium and Holland to Hitler's home turf.

One point of pride the Canadians could take into battle with them was the realization that they were fighting for a nation that had ceased to be considered a mere colony of Great Britain. A few days before June 6, General Crerar presented all Canadian units with a new Canadian flag, the Red Ensign, as their battle standard. No longer would Canadian troops head into battle under the Union Jack.

# Chapter 4
# D-Day: The Normandy Invasion

**R**umours were rife amongst the Allied troops assembled in Southern England in the late spring of 1944. Every scenario being fed to the Germans by Allied counter-intelligence, and then leaked out to the men in the ranks, was chewed over. And, soldiers being soldiers, they also had their own home-made theories about when and where the cross-Channel attack would take place.

The murmurings came to a head when the troops lined up to get their pay packets on May 27. Each soldier received 10 shillings in silver, which, as usual, was to be used to buy small personal items in England. But they also found 200 francs in paper currency in their pay envelopes. This could mean only one thing: before another payday rolled around, they would be in France. But as May 31 approached — the revised date for the attack — Allied meteorologists forecast the worst spring weather in the English Channel in the past 20 years. The military strategists therefore were forced to move D-Day to June 5. This decision caused some sleepless nights for the Allied Supreme Command because the tide tables revealed that conditions for a successful landing were slipping away, and the next suitable set of dates would be sometime in August — a long time to keep Operation Overlord under wraps.

Despite deteriorating weather on June 3, Allied Supreme Commander General Dwight D. Eisenhower, an American Army career officer, ordered the invasion force to begin boarding the assault ships. For the troops, this meant two days and nights in cramped, foul-smelling, and wind-buffeted vessels that would remain in port until the signal to leave on June 5, but everything had to be in readiness when the attack order was issued.

Unfortunately, June 5 promised to be another day of wicked weather, with high winds and choppy seas in the Channel that would prevent the invasion force from getting ashore — provided the whole flotilla wasn't swamped in the crossing. This left General Eisenhower no alternative but to delay the attack for another 24 hours in the hope that the weather would improve. Needless to say, the nerve-jangled soldiers indulged in a great deal of grumbling and cursing.

These troops had been rehearsing the attack for more than two years, and were primed for getting on with it, but they would have to stay jammed together for another 24 hours on ships that were anything but luxury liners.

General Eisenhower and his senior staff were probably no happier than their disappointed troops as they watched the hours inch by without a break in the weather. Finally, at 0415 hours on the morning of June 5, Eisenhower grasped at a meteorological straw — his weather forecasters pinned a slight hope on a break in the weather over the Channel in the early hours of June 6. The Supreme Commander stared out the rain-lashed windows of his Portsmouth headquarters for a few moments, took a deep breath, and muttered, "Okay, we'll go."

**Letter Of Encouragement**

To rally his troops, Eisenhower issued the following text on Supreme Headquarters Allied Expeditionary Force (SHAEF) letterhead:

> *Soldiers, Sailors and Airmen of the Allied Expeditionary Force!*
>
> *You are about to embark upon the Great Crusade, toward which we have striven these many months. The eyes of the world are upon you. The hopes and prayers of liberty-loving people everywhere march with you. In company with our brave Allies and brothers-in-arms on other Fronts, you will bring about the destruction of the*

*German war machine, the elimination of Nazi tyranny over the oppressed peoples of Europe, and security for ourselves in a free world.*

*Your task will not be an easy one. Your enemy is well trained, well equipped and battle-hardened. He will fight savagely.*

*But this is the year 1944! Much has happened since the Nazi triumphs of 1940-41. The United Nations have inflicted upon the Germans great defeats, in open battle, man-to-man. Our air offensive has seriously reduced their strength in the air and their capacity to wage war on the ground. Our Home Fronts have given us an overwhelming superiority in weapons and munitions of war, and placed at our disposal great reserves of trained fighting men. The tide has turned! The free men of the world are marching together to Victory!*

*I have full confidence in your courage, devotion to duty and skill in battle. We will accept nothing less than full Victory!*

*Good Luck! And let us all beseech the blessing of Almighty God upon this great and noble undertaking.*

*Dwight Eisenhower*

**The Enemy Awaits**

Hitler hadn't called the coastal defences of Northern France "The Atlantic Wall" for nothing. In the spring of 1942, Der Führer had ordered the construction of minefields, concrete walls, concrete bunkers, tank traps, barbed wire fences, and fortified artillery emplacements to ring the 4800-kilometre coast.

The Normandy region, which had up until this point been considered the rear area for Eastern Front troops to rest and refit, soon bristled with such weaponry as the powerful 88mm anti-tank/anti-aircraft gun, and tanks such as the Panther and Tiger, which were considered superior to Allied armour.

When General Rommel was appointed commander of the area in 1943, he considered the defences to be still woefully inadequate and set about to strengthen them, laying in more minefields right down to the beach and into the water to be concealed by high tide. He redoubled the efforts to put obstacles in the path of any invading army, and added some of his own embellishments, such as sharp wooden stakes and gigantic steel tetrahedrons (like something out of a giant child's game of Jacks). He increased the number of machine-gun nests and mortar pits, as well as steel-and-concrete-reinforced pillboxes.

In addition, Rommel opened up dams and weirs to send water cascading onto flood plains behind the beaches, and fields were inundated with long poles sticking high up into the air to deter the landing of airplanes and gliders.

Rommel wrote at the time that he knew the defences he'd been put in charge of building wouldn't stop an invasion force. He felt the best he could hope for was to delay the invasion and prevent the assault force from gaining a foothold, since once they were established, it would open the door to limitless Allied resources pouring into France. His defensive plans involved defeating the Allies on the beaches by bringing in reserve troops to back up the mixed bag of soldiers he had inherited. The current lot included everything from seasoned troops from the Eastern Front to captured Russians who'd been given the choice of fighting for Germany or being executed by totally green Hitler Jugend (Youth), a hastily conscripted unit of teenagers who made up for a lack of experience with their fanatical zeal to serve Der Führer.

The thing that disturbed Rommel and his general staff most — other than the growing realization that they were serving a madman — was that they had no idea where the invasion force would land. With Hitler's insistence on keeping crack troops in reserve all over Europe in case of a massive attack at any of a number of potential targets, German manpower and materiel was spread dangerously thin within Fortress Europe.

**Launching The Attack**

The RCAF followed up on months of bombing strategic enemy targets in the Normandy region by flying as part of a contingent of some 170 Allied squadrons that participated in the D-Day operations. As H-Hour approached, RCAF Lancaster aircraft of No. 6 Bomber Group dropped thousands of tons of explosives on Nazi defences. RAF and United States Air Force (USAF) aircraft would also pound the invasion beaches unmercifully in the hours before the first assault troops arrived.

Canadian fighter pilots helped the Allies obtain air superiority by knocking their Luftwaffe counterparts out of the skies. They would also play a decisive role in protecting Allied soldiers on the invasion beaches and in destroying German troops and gun emplacements. By D-Day, there were three RCAF Spitfire wings in Europe, plus a wing of ground-attack Typhoons and a reconnaissance wing of Spitfires and Mustangs.

Once the Allied beachhead had been established, the first Allied aircraft to operate from the newly liberated French soil would be RCAF squadrons No. 441, 442, and 443.

The Royal Canadian Navy (RCN) contributed about 110 vessels and some 10,000 sailors to the 5333 craft in the invasion fleet, code-named Operation Neptune. The entire armada was made up of 931 ships transporting the assault troops and equipment to the two western U.S. beaches, and 1796 ships for the three British and Canadian beaches.

There were 2727 vessels in all, including 137 warships that would bombard the German defences. The landing ships carried a total of 176,475 men and 21,651 vehicles, as well as 2600 landing craft.

Sixteen Canadian minesweepers took part in the essential task of clearing away floating bombs in the English

D-Day landing ships carried a total of 176,475 men.

Channel in advance of the invasion force. Navy frogmen also played a decisive role in reconnoitring beaches and removing whatever obstacles they could. The destroyers HMCS *Sioux* and HMCS *Algonquin* were assigned the task of leading the way to Juno Beach, then bombarding enemy defences to soften them up for the Canadian invaders.

Fourteen assault landing craft were carried in the landing ships, the armed merchant cruisers *Prince David* and *Prince Henry*, while six RCN motor torpedo boats patrolled off the Seine estuary. Dozens of corvettes and frigates patrolled the convoy routes of the invading forces and escorted landing craft and barges to the beach area.

In all, 5 Allied battleships, 2 monitors, 19 cruisers, 77 destroyers, and 2 gunboats joined their RAF, USAF, and RCAF airborne counterparts in shelling the Normandy beaches. And, as the armada got closer to shore, the artillery pieces located on landing craft and barges would add their firepower to the melee. On the Canadian front, four self-propelled regiments each took on one target.

The first Allied combat troops arrived in Nazi-Occupied France shortly after midnight. They were the 13,400 paratroopers and glider-borne soldiers of the 82nd and 101st U.S. Airborne, and the 6250 British and Canadian paratroopers in the British 6th Airborne.

Their orders were to seize strategic objectives inland from the beaches, particularly bridges, to prevent German reinforcements from rushing to the invasion area. They were also expected to help the beach invaders move to their inland targets as quickly as possible.

The plan was to drop the U.S. 82nd Airborne Division on both banks of the Merderet River, south and west of Ste-Mère-Église, which was north of Carentan on a strategic road access the Germans would need to send reinforcements to the Cotentin Peninsula. The 101st Airborne's mission was to capture the transportation link to Utah, the westernmost landing beach, and the crossings of the Douve River.

The British 6th Airborne Division, which included 450

Canadians, had orders to jump or land in gliders on the eastern bank of the Orne River, northeast of Caen, to guard the left flank of Sword Beach.

The pilots of the C-47 transport aircraft carrying the American paratroopers were inexperienced at such tasks and overreacted to the flak from German anti-aircraft guns. Also hampered by high winds and an unexpected cloudbank, the C-47 pilots took evasive action that dropped their human cargo in the wrong places, some into flooded areas where they drowned, and some into enemy gun emplacements around Ste-Mère-Église.

**Wrong Drop Zone**

In the epic movie about D-Day, *The Longest Day* (an expression borrowed from Field Marshal Rommel), a climactic scene shows actor Red Buttons, in full combat gear, hanging by his parachute straps from the steeple of the church at Ste-Mère-Église. As the scene ends, Red's eyes widen as, off-camera, the sound of a German rifle bolt clicking into place can be heard.

That scene is based on an actual event, although dramatized for effect. The real paratrooper, Private John Steele of the U.S. 82nd Airborne Division, dangled from the steeple for two hours, feigning death while in terrible pain from a shattered foot that had been hit by flak during his descent. He was eventually cut down and taken prisoner by the Germans. He reportedly died in Kentucky in 1969. Today, visitors to the village do a double-take when they see a dummy paratrooper hanging from the steeple in commemoration of the event.

Although their landings were a fiasco, the U.S. paratroopers managed to regroup on the ground to some extent, and ad hoc units were able to salvage most of the invasion plan.

The British and Canadian paratroopers also ran into difficulties. Their transport pilots, buffeted by high winds and experiencing navigational difficulties, made ill-timed drops that saw many of their charges jumping from about 300 feet into rivers, trees, and swamps. Weighted down by heavy gear, a number of paratroopers drowned.

In spite of it all, the Brits and Canadians succeeded in seizing the bridges over the Orne and the Caen Canal. They destroyed enemy installations at Merville and blew up bridges over the Dives River to the east.

Setting up a defensive position on the high ground between the two rivers around Varaville, they now waited for their comrades to take Juno Beach and begin the push inland.

# Chapter 5
# H-Hour For Canada

The Canadian assault troops in the ports of Southern England had been cooped up in cramped quarters aboard the landing ships for the better — or worse — part of three days. Veterans of the campaign have revealed how relieved they were when they finally felt the ships' engines begin to throb and the landscape slowly start to slip away.

Leonard W. Brockingham, aboard HMCS *Sioux*, overheard one senior British naval officer say: "What Philip of Spain tried to do and failed, what Napoleon had wanted to do and could not, what Hitler never had the courage to attempt, we are about to do and with God's grace, we shall succeed."

Once beyond the protective headlands of the English

coast, the ships began to wallow in the high chop of a storm-ravaged English Channel. Heavy clouds blackened the skies. The ships plowed through high winds, heavy seas, and driving rain. Seasickness became the immediate enemy. Many a documentary or written account of the crossing contains vivid descriptions of how queasy the men were. They complained openly that they didn't care if they had to face the whole blankety-blank German Army — all they wanted to do was get off the ship and wade ashore to dry land. It seemed like a good idea at the time.

Four Canadian soldiers in one of the landing ships figured that the two ounces of Navy rum doled out to each of them to ward off the chill — or the fear of going into battle — wouldn't carry them very far. One of them had a deck of cards, so they dumped all eight ounces of liquor into one cup, then cut cards for the whole lot, with high card taking all. The first soldier cut a three, much to the amusement of his comrades — who one after the other proceeded to cut a deuce.

Unfortunately for the seemingly lucky soldier, due to the heavy seas in the Channel, the rum and the man's breakfast later ended up being tossed over the side of a landing craft in a vomit bag thoughtfully supplied by the RCN for that purpose.

What the troops didn't know as they neared the French coast was that the comforting racket of shelling from the Allied destroyers and the drone of Allied bombers overhead on their way to Normandy targets was lulling them into a feeling of false security. So solidly built were the German bunkers and artillery batteries that many of them are still standing today. This meant the enemy wouldn't be nearly as softened up as the assault strategists had expected.

Another problem that quickly became apparent was that the amphibious DD tanks, sporting high canvas flotation screens and propellers to push them, were not going to be as effective as the military planners had hoped. This floating armour was supposed to be launched ahead of the troops and make its way to the beaches to blast out pockets of enemy troops that hadn't been blown away by the aerial and naval bombing.

Unfortunately, in their haste to get the DDs ashore, the invasion co-ordinators ordered a number of them launched too far out from the coast and the tanks foundered in the five-foot depths. They had been built to navigate in water no deeper than four feet. Those tanks that were successfully launched were often so slow that landing craft actually passed them on the way to the beach. In parts of the British and Canadian sectors, rough seas led to the decision not to launch the tanks at all, but to wait until they could be offloaded directly onto the beach.

The British and Canadian troops didn't need these glitches. Their situation was already tough enough. Because of underwater rock formations, they could not land until one and a half hours after dawn, when the tide was high enough to provide clearance for the landing craft over the rocks and

German-laid obstacles. This delay meant that the Nazi defenders would have been alerted that an invasion was underway by the earlier-launched American assault. The Nazis would be waiting to throw everything they had at the British and Canadian troops.

### Stormy Weather Helps

The bad weather in the Channel actually helped the Allied necessity for surprise. Alexander McKee wrote in *Caen: Anvil of Victory*: "The Germans expected a landing in the Pas de Calais, but the invaders were steering for Normandy. They were expected at high tide and (the first invaders) would land at low. They were expected in calm weather and not when the breakers were roaring on the beaches. German meteorologists had concluded there would be no invasion for at least two weeks and most German commanders accepted that."

In fact, many of the officers had decided to spend a few days on leave. Rommel, for instance, went home for a quick visit with his family.

But the first inkling the Germans got that something was afoot actually came when SHAEF beamed a British Broadcasting Corporation (BBC) message to the people of France at 2115 hours on the night of June 5. The alert suggested that in due course instructions of great importance would be given through that radio channel and that they must listen at all hours.

This warning to the French tipped off the Germans that

something big was about to happen. In addition, Nazi-operated radar stations between Cherbourg and Le Havre reported that they were being jammed. Stations from Fécamp to Calais reported abnormally heavy shipping in the Channel.

Between 2200 hours and 2300 hours, Luftwaffe Signals Intelligence noted that reconnaissance aircraft for American bombers were broadcasting weather information. German night fighters were told to stand by for further instructions.

At 2200 hours, Rommel's Army Group Headquarters (HQ) issued a most urgent signal to all troops to be ready for action. But so ingrained in the German psyche was the belief that the invasion would take place at the Pas de Calais, that this alert was directed to the 15th Army only, with its divisions to the north and east of Normandy. There was no alarm sent to the German 7th Army, guarding the coast that was soon to feel the brunt of the Allied invasion fleet.

**Into The Fray**
On Mike sector of Juno Beach, most of the 1st Hussars' tanks got ashore and were able to provide covering fire as The Regina Rifles' landing craft scraped bottom and the troops came charging out just after 0800 hours. The Hussars had their work cut out for them because the naval and aerial bombardment had had little effect on the German defensive positions.

The solid concrete bunkers, averaging 35 feet across with walls 4 feet thick, could only be knocked out by direct

Canadian Tank crews removing water-proofing from their tanks,
Normandy Beachhead.

hits through their observation slits. This did happen on several occasions, due to the accuracy of tank crews and the bravery of individual Regina personnel who faced withering fire to get close enough to toss hand grenades through the openings.

Tanks and infantry fought their way off the beach and into the target village of Courseulles-sur-Mer, at the mouth of the Seulles River, where they faced off against determined German troops in house-to-house combat. By late afternoon, they had moved inland.

One Regina Rifles officer liked to tell the story later about riding through a potato patch behind a house in Courseulles in a tracked vehicle. An old French gentleman came running out of the house, shells flying all around him. Shaking his fist, the old man proceeded to dress down the Canadians for what they had done to his potato patch.

Overall, the Canadian invasion was going so well that by 1030 hours, Juno Beach Commander Major General Keller felt confident enough to send a message to General Crerar: "Beachhead gained. Well on our way to our immediate objectives." As it turned out, this euphoria was a bit premature.

The diary of one of the Reginas perhaps describes best how a great many of the French civilians greeted the invasion forces, who, after all, were destroying their property. Many of the troops had expressed uneasiness at how the civilians would react. The diary relates: "1100 hours. Civilians of Courseulles welcomed our troops with flowers. Old men and women, young girls and children, stood in the littered streets, clapped their hands, waved at the troops, and tossed roses in their path. A girl handed me a crimson rose and there were tears of despair and joy in her eyes: 'There's my home over there; ruined. But the Allies are here.'"

Other members of the Reginas weren't as lucky as those who advanced inland into the welcome arms of the French civilians. A reserve company sustained terrible losses when their landing craft struck underwater mines concealed by the high tide.

# D-Day

Also making it ashore on Mike sector were the company of Canadian Scottish (CanScots) and most of the contingent of The Royal Winnipeg Rifles. In their case, spot-on naval gunnery had destroyed the German battery that had been defending that section of the beach.

## Bombardment Off Target

Things didn't go so well for the Winnipeg company that landed on sand dunes at the western edge of Courseulles. The naval and aerial bombardments had been off target and the landing craft came under withering fire while still a considerable distance offshore. The invaders were forced to jump into chest-deep water, and their slow movement toward the beaches made them easy pickings for enemy rifles and machine guns. Although the survivors eventually managed to overtake the beach defences, clear the minefields, and occupy the nearby coastal villages, the company lost almost three-quarters of its men within a few hours.

The Winnipegs' commanding officer later had high praise for the tank crews of the 1st Hussars, citing their "gallantry, skill and cool daring" in coming to the aid of his battalion "time and again throughout D-Day, without thought of their own safety or state of fatigue..."

To their credit, whenever veterans gather and begin to tell stories of the hardship of battle, someone will inevitably attempt to lighten things up by relating a humorous incident that took place.

For instance, one D-Day invader tells of a signaller on a landing craft who saw his company commander step into chest-deep water and decided to jump in beside him. The commander was six foot one, and the signaller was five feet, four inches. He almost drowned and his radio was swamped, but he managed to make it safely to shore.

At Nan sector, The North Shore (New Brunswick) Regiment, whose objective was the resort village of St-Aubin, and The Queen's Own Rifles, targeting Bernières-sur-Mer, also had trouble with German gun emplacements that had escaped the naval and aerial bombing. One concrete bunker in particular was responsible for inflicting heavy casualties on the Canadians. It also destroyed several Sherman tanks of The Fort Garry Horse before the advancing troops were able to put it out of commission.

Despite the heavy firing, the war diary of The Queen's Own Rifles reports that at 0900 hours, a café 90 metres off the beach in Bernières was open and selling wine. And radio newscaster Marcel Ouimet of the Canadian Broadcasting Corporation (CBC), who went in with the troops, described the scene to his listeners. "We found a little inn called l'Hôtel Belle Plage — it's now l'Hôtel du Régiment de la Chaudière — owned by a most hospitable man who had a reserve of the native brew and he dished it out pretty freely. Some Canadians didn't realize that calvados is stronger than even whisky blanc. A few took too much and we only found them a couple of days later."

The North Shores' remaining companies were able to get ashore without any problems, but heavy concentrations of enemy fire slowed them down to the point where it took six hours for them to secure the town of Tailleville, with armoured support. One of their number, Lance Corporal Bud Daley, came across the body of his own brother. He retrieved some personal belongings and a few things to send home, then had to push on.

**Queen's Own Hit Hard**
Because the early shelling from RCN ships and RCAF bombers had had little effect on German defences in their sector of Nan, The Queen's Own Rifles fared the worst of any Canadian unit that day. Delayed for half an hour by bad weather and rough seas, the troops stormed ashore into brutal enemy fire from a hidden 88mm gun that wiped out two-thirds of the lead platoon. With only an exposed beach between them and a sea wall almost 200 metres away, most of the surviving members of that Queen's Own unit were mowed down, and only a few were left alive to proceed inland.

Where they might have been helped by the amphibious DD tanks, high waves had slowed the armour down and had forced them to land in the line of fire of the beach defence guns. Most of the tanks were destroyed, their high-explosive shells blowing off their armour plating from within, and lubricating oil and rubber accessories turning these flaming torches into smouldering tombs for the trapped crews.

A second Queen's Own company hit the beach directly in front of an enemy strongpoint that had emerged unscathed from the earlier bombardment. Half the unit was lost before three riflemen managed to get close enough to the German fortification to silence it with grenades and small arms fire.

The official diary of the Queen's Own relates a strange coincidence that took place during the landings:

"The probability that our two first-wave assault companies would be commanded by brothers was rather remote, but so it was. Both Daltons had been in the regiment in militia days.

"Major Charles Dalton: 'People ask how we decided whose company would go in on the right and whose on the left. We tossed a coin and I think my brother felt there should be a farewell scene. Something from Hamlet, maybe. Something appropriate. Instead, we shook hands, said good luck and went to our boats.'

"Major Elliot Dalton: 'We were weaving among the obstacles and mines and just before we touched down, we leaned over to tell the coxswain to go slightly to the right — only to find he'd been hit between the eyes and was dead. The craft had weaved in on its own. Of the 10 boats, we were the only one that didn't hit a mine.'

"Major Charles Dalton: 'We thought we were on the beach. Really, we were hooked on an underwater obstacle.

The doors went down and I very gallantly shouted: 'Follow me!' and disappeared in eight feet of water. The fire was heavy and almost every man on my right was wounded or killed. I'd have been hit too but we found later that the machine gun that was doing the damage couldn't traverse that far. The man next to me was hit four or five times. I wasn't touched.'"

The coincidences surrounding the Dalton brothers didn't end there. Sustaining a head wound in the D-Day attack, Major Charles Dalton was evacuated to England and placed in a hospital ward with a dozen or so fellow Canadian wounded. The patient in the bed next to him was being discharged as Charles was wheeled into the operating room. To his astonishment, when he woke up after his operation, the new patient in the next bed, his leg encased in plaster to mend bones broken in a mortar attack, was Major Elliot Dalton.

Both Dalton brothers later received the Distinguished Service Order for their heroic actions during the Normandy operation.

**Second Wave Launched**
The reserve units of the CanScots and Le Régiment de la Chaudière came in on the second wave of the D-Day attack. The CanScots found themselves in the fortunate position of facing the least resistance and thus suffered the lightest casualties of any Canadian battalion that day. One of their

D-Day's beach landings required new landing craft technology.

number wrote in his diary: "Hordes of prisoners were taken and our advance was too rapid to do anything but disarm them and send them to the beach cage (set up for captured enemy soldiers) under one or two escorts. The odd prisoner tried to escape, but will never have that opportunity again."

On the other hand, there were German troops who wanted desperately to surrender. On one of the beaches, two riflemen made a wrong turn while bringing up petrol and found themselves in a small enemy pocket. Five Germans came running up and offered 4500 francs if they could be taken prisoner. The two Canadians tumbled the Germans onto the truck, turned around, and delivered the five to a prisoner-of-war cage. They split the money and made their way, petrol intact, back to their unit.

The unit of Chaudières hitting the beaches on the second wave had a bit of a rough ride. On the rising tide, many of their landing craft struck underwater explosives and, since the troops were still too far out in the Channel to wade ashore, they had to jettison their equipment and swim for it. A number of them drowned in the attempt. Both regiments, however, managed to get off the beach quickly and head inland.

By late afternoon, the Chaudières were able to take the town of Beny-sur-Mer, thanks to effective support from the destroyer *Algonquin* just offshore.

A member of the Canscots, who was also involved in the taking of Beny-sur-Mer, later told of seeing troops waiting for orders to advance on the village, a rifle in one hand and a French phrase book in the other — much to the amusement of local inhabitants. Upon entering Beny, it was the Canadians' turn to be amused. The Germans had hardly left before the locals began to loot their barracks. Even the parish priest was seen with a set of dishes.

## Gigantic Traffic Jam

By noon, all units of the 3rd Canadian Infantry Division had landed at Juno Beach, and the 9th Infantry Brigade was able to head ashore to capitalize on this success. However, a traffic jam had occurred at Bernières. The beach and streets were clogged with troops and bicycles, trucks and tanks, all trying to move through the narrow roadways. It was 1500 hours before anything could move further inland. That congestion is blamed to a great extent for the Canadians not reaching their final D-Day objectives.

In a late afternoon counterattack, about 40 tanks of the Germans' 21st Panzer Division tried to break through to the coast between the Canadian and 3rd British Divisions, but the Allies stopped them literally in their tracks. Another group of German tanks got close to the beach around Luc-sur-Mer but met fierce opposition. Thanks to heavy Allied firepower in the air, a very dangerous German tank division that would later wreak havoc on the Canadians — the 12th SS Panzers — stayed under cover and saw no action on D-Day.

Another incident of that luck of the draw that old soldiers often refer to proved to be a fortunate event for one naïve soldier once the Canadians had established a foothold on the D-Day beaches. An artillery sergeant was ordered to cross an open stretch of terrain to alert another battery that they were shelling a two-storey building that housed Canadian wounded on the ground floor. The other battery's radio had been knocked out and although they were trying to eliminate a German machine-gun nest in the upper portion of the house, they were unaware of the Canadians below. The sergeant ambled across the open field and was surprised to see puffs of dirt flying up all around him since he couldn't figure out how raindrops could be stirring up the soil on a cloudless day. Only when he got to the other battery did he learn that the "raindrops" were actually German machine-gun bullets kicking up the dust all around him.

By nightfall, the Canadian forward units were in sight of Caen, and two battalions were only five kilometres from the city's northwestern outskirts. On the right, the 7th Brigade linked up with the 50th British Division, forming a common beachhead 20 kilometres wide and 10 to 11 kilometres deep. But on the left, there was still a strip of enemy-held territory between the 3rd Canadian and the 3rd British Division.

Late in the day, the Highland Regiment captured Colombiers-sur-Seulles, and a troop of 1st Hussars tanks, commanded by Lieutenant W.F. McCormick, advanced 15 kilometres from the beach to the vicinity of the Caen-Bayeux Highway intersection. They gained the reputation of being the only Allied unit to capture their planned final objective on D-Day.

McCormick described to the CBC how, after helping The Winnipeg Rifles through Creully, they had pushed to the north edge of Secqueville-en-Bessin. They came to a crossroads and a German soldier sauntered up to them thinking they were one of his. No one had expected to see the enemy that far inland.

The British and Americans had managed to get ashore with varying degrees of difficulty. The U.S. 4th Infantry Division took Utah Beach on the lower end of the Cotentin Peninsula with relative ease. But on Omaha Beach, the U.S. 1st Infantry Division had the bloodiest landing of all. The unlucky GIs hit a stretch of beach controlled by German gun batteries that were well dug in on the high ground.

Gold and Sword Beaches were attacked by the British 50th and 8th Infantry Divisions, and the 3rd Infantry Division and 22nd Armoured Brigade respectively. The landings took place under heavy German resistance that slowed the assault forces enough for them to fail to take their D-Day objective of Caen.

The Canadian landings, despite tragic losses that were still fewer than the military strategists had predicted, were a great success. By the evening of D-Day, Canadian troops had progressed farther inland than any unit of their Allies.

When the final tally was taken, some 350 Canadians had paid the supreme sacrifice on D-Day. Close to 600 others had been wounded, and about 50 or so had been taken prisoner. To this day, these statistics are only estimates because conditions on the D-Day beaches prevented an exact compilation. One medical breakthrough kept the fatalities from skyrocketing. Penicillin had become readily available in 1944, and it is estimated that 12 to 15 percent of the wounded would have died of infection without it.

Between 7 and 10 percent of Allied casualties were caused by the large number of land mines sewn by the Wehrmacht. Small shoe mines were just large enough to blow off a man's foot. This was considered an economical way of tying up several other men to care for and evacuate the wounded soldier.

The more lethal "S" mine, referred to with defiant cheekiness by the Allied soldier as the "Bouncing Betty," featured a propellant charge that fired it about four feet into the air before the main charge detonated, sending shrapnel in all directions. It needed only seven pounds of ground pressure to set it off.

**Air Superiority**

Military historians agree that the toll of Canadian, British, and American casualties would have been much greater were it not for the superiority in the air that the Allies enjoyed. Allied bombers and fighters, wrote Chester Wilmot in *The Struggle for Europe*, flew 10,585 sorties on D-Day, in addition to the 1730 flown by transport planes in airborne operations. Not a single aircraft was lost through Luftwaffe intervention. There was little sign of the German air force over the beaches until almost dark, when four Henkels surreptitiously managed to scatter their bomb loads near the Canadian beaches. RAF Spitfires pounced on them and none survived to fly another mission. There was one other report of two Focke-Wulf (FW) 190 fighters making a single, ineffective pass over the beaches.

By the same token, the German Kriegsmarine had offered no resistance. The only Allied ship lost was a Norwegian destroyer that had been sunk by a floating mine. By this late in the war, earlier Allied victories in the Battle of the Atlantic, coupled with a shortage of fuel and parts for the German Navy, had made this once-proud fleet a mere shadow of its former self.

The first day of Operation Overlord, by all accounts, had been an outstanding success. The British and Americans had also captured their respective beaches and advanced inland. By the end of the day, the Allies had landed some 155,000 troops in Nazi-Occupied France, along with a vast cache of weapons and supplies.

On the down side, lousy weather conditions, a less-than-perfect pre-raid bombardment, strong defensive fortifications, German troops who were more skilled and determined than anticipated, and an overly optimistic battle plan prevented the Allies from taking most of their D-Day objectives.

Still, the Atlantic Wall had been penetrated, and Hitler's Fortress Europe was in greater peril than it had been since the outbreak of war. The Allies had secured a foothold in France and, with the imminent arrival of the artificial harbours and the rapid installation of makeshift airfields, troops and supplies would continue to pour into Normandy at an impressive rate.

But no one was naïve enough to think that things would

be easy from that point forward. The Germans had been fooled into thinking Normandy was only a secondary target and had therefore neglected to send in their formidable reserves. Now that it was known that Normandy was the main thrust of the Allied invasion of Europe, a furious Führer realized his Third Reich was in a fight to the death. The bloodbath had just begun.

## Chapter 6
# The Germans Counterattack

The Germans didn't waste much time in launching their anticipated counterattack. On June 7 — D plus one — the Canadian units continued their push inland. The Royal Winnipeg Rifles and The Regina Rifles had little trouble in reaching their original D-Day objective — the Caen-Bayeux Highway. However, their jubilation at this accomplishment would be short-lived.

Elsewhere, it was the job of the 9th Brigade's North Nova Scotia Highlanders, supported by the armour of The Sherbrooke Fusiliers, to push for the Carpiquet airfield, about five kilometres west of Caen. So rapid was their advance that they got beyond the range of Canadian artillery support, and naval gunfire was temporarily not available because of radio failure.

To make matters worse, there were no Allied troops on the Canadians' left. A British brigade that was supposed to be there had been re-routed to another area under attack. Nor could the Canadians make contact with any support troops to their right.

Battle-hardened German Panzer troops were waiting for the Canadians as they entered the village of Buron, and bloody house-to-house fighting took place before the Nazi troops were driven out.

Because they were ahead of artillery support, the Canadians headed into a trap in the next village on their rapid advance towards Carpiquet. Having escaped Canadian shelling, the village of Authie, which was heavily fortified with concrete bunkers, was teeming with a mixed bag of German troops. This was the soon-to-be-infamous 12th Panzer Division, a ruthless formation of untested but fanatic Hitler Jugend led by experienced officers and non-commissioned officers (NCOs) from the Russian Front, under the command of Standartenführer (Colonel) Kurt Meyer.

The Nazi officer had spotted the Novas and Fusiliers entering the village from the church tower of the Abbey at nearby Ardenne. From his lofty perch, Meyer was able to train his binoculars on one tank that stopped only 180 metres from where some of Meyer's men were hidden behind a hedge. On his orders, not a shot was fired.

A Canadian armoured unit then emerged from Buron

after mopping up pockets of Germans who had refused to surrender. The tanks were heading for the Caen-Bayeux Highway, but were unwittingly moving across the front of Meyer's well-hidden Second Battalion, exposing a long, unprotected flank.

## Superior Panzer Armour

As the Canadian armour neared the highway, Meyer yelled "Attack!" and all hell broke loose. The leading Canadian tank was blown up, then the second. Tank after tank succumbed to the superior firepower of the Panzer armour, while shells from the Canadian Sherman tanks bounced off the Panzers like ping-pong balls.

The relatively green Canadians, the vast majority of whom just days before had been untested in battle, had never seen anything like these give-no-quarter Nazis. What followed was a series of atrocities that to this day enrages any Canadian veteran who witnessed them or even heard second, third, or fourth-hand accounts.

In the early stages of the Authie encounter, C Company of the North Novas was wiped out, and after prolonged hand-to-hand fighting, the Canadians withdrew. Their casualties totalled nearly 250 North Nova Scotia Highlanders and some 60 Fusiliers, killed or captured in a battle tantalizingly close to the city of Caen.

On June 8, the SS struck again. German tanks and infantry surrounded and annihilated three forward companies of The Royal Winnipeg Rifles at Putot-en-Bessin. That evening, The Canadian Scottish and tanks from the 1st Hussars managed to recapture the town, but at a heavy cost.

The Regina Rifles were also battered, with 22 German tanks encircling battalion headquarters. A night-long battle ensued. As the regiment's war diary recorded: "The whole sky was lit up by blazing roofs and burning tanks. Everyone fought magnificently and although the picture looked black, there was no sign of wavering anywhere." Like the cavalry of a low-budget western movie, The Sherbrooke Fusiliers arrived just in time to salvage a desperate situation, aided by the Reginas making good use of the infantry's anti-tank weapon, the PIAT.

In two days, the young and virtually inexperienced Canadians had learned a grim lesson. The North Novas, Winnipegs, Sherbrookes, and Scottish sustained close to 600 casualties. But they held the more experienced German troops to a standstill.

As with any battle, there were many examples of quiet courage in the Normandy fighting. One poignant account of devotion to duty involved Rifleman Gilbert D. Boxall of Canwood, Saskatchewan, who, as a member of The Regina Rifles Regiment, was killed at Beny-sur-Mer on June 9.

Rifleman Boxall landed on Juno Beach on June 6 as a stretcher-bearer. He gave first aid on the beach and in the battle inland. On D plus three, running to a soldier he heard calling for help, he was cut down and killed. On his body were found five dried shell dressings — he suffered five wounds prior to being killed. He never said a word to anybody, just crawled away somewhere, put a dressing on his wound, and went back into the fray to help his fellow Canadians.

On June 11, the Canadians went at it again, with little to show for it. Fighting alongside British units, members of Le Régiment de la Chaudière and The Fort Garry Horse slugged it out with SS troops in the town of Rots, which the Allies eventually took.

Their comrades in The Queen's Own Rifles and the 1st Hussar weren't as fortunate. Their attack on the village of Le Mesnil-Patry — one of the objectives taken by the 1st Canadian Parachute Battalion on D-Day but subsequently abandoned — saw them come under heavy fire from well-entrenched German artillery and armour. Nineteen Sherman tanks from the lead squadron of the Hussars were destroyed and only two escaped the devastating fire of the Nazi 88mm guns. When the smoke had cleared, the two regiments suffered combined casualties of 114 killed and 65 wounded.

While battles were raging on the ground, other life-and-death struggles were occurring at sea and in the air. For instance, another Canadian Victoria Cross was won on June 12 — this one by RCAF Pilot Officer Andrew Charles Mynarski of Winnipeg. He was the mid-upper gunner of a Lancaster on a night mission to bomb a target in Cambrai, France. The aircraft was attacked by an enemy fighter and erupted in flames.

The captain ordered the crew to bail out, and Pilot

# D-Day

Officer Mynarski was about to do so when he noticed the rear gunner trapped in his turret. With disregard for his own safety, and with his parachute and flying suit in flames, Mynarski attempted to release the rear gunner. Unable to free the trapped crewmember, Pilot Officer Mynarski, his gear and clothing still ablaze, leapt from the plane, but not before turning to his trapped comrade and saluting him. Mynarski landed safely, but later died of his burns. The rear gunner had a miraculous escape when the bomber crashed, and lived to tell the story.

Another tail gunner, this one a crewmember of a Halifax bomber, also had a miraculous escape from his crippled aircraft. Ordered to bail out, he found himself dangling upside down outside the turret, his flying boots wedged in the twisted metal from the damaged aircraft. With the plane ready to explode at any moment, the airman pulled his feet from his boots, yanked his parachute's ripcord, and landed safely — right in a courtyard near a German outpost.

Picking himself up and extricating himself from his chute, the Canadian marched swiftly by two German soldiers, who saluted him, apparently thinking he was a senior officer from another branch of the service. It was only when they looked down at his stockinged feet that they realized something was amiss. The Canadian airman spent the rest of the war in a prison camp.

After six days of bloody fighting, the now-seasoned soldiers of the 3rd Canadian Division and the 2nd Armoured

Brigade had suffered losses of over 1000 dead and nearly 2000 wounded. But they had at last captured their D-Day objectives.

As the CBC's Matthew Halton told his audience on June 20: "The Canadians were new to battle. They'd never heard the screaming shrapnel before. They hadn't been machine-gunned or sniped at. They hadn't had bombs thrown in their faces. They hadn't been overrun in their slit trenches by tanks. But they have now."

Unfortunately, there was one other bitter lesson the Canadians would learn: man's inhumanity to man — personified in the strutting arrogance and cold-blooded cruelty of a stocky beer salesman named Kurt Meyer.

### SS Atrocities

In war, fatalities are expected and accepted as the price of doing battle. But under the Geneva Convention, those military personnel taken prisoner are to be treated fairly and safeguarded until the end of hostilities or until such time as a prisoner swap can be arranged. Apparently, nobody told that to Standartenführer Kurt Meyer.

The Allies were later able to document that between June 7 and June 17, 134 Canadian prisoners of war from various units were murdered by the 12th Panzer Division of SS misfits and teenaged Hitler Youth under Meyer's command. That's 134 documented cases. The belief is that there were many more instances of the slaughter of the innocents that couldn't be proven.

The first Canadians to die at the hands of their Nazi captors were some of the men of The North Nova Scotia Highlanders and The Sherbrooke Fusiliers, taken prisoner at the battle of Authie. They were paraded with their hands behind their heads into the Abbey gardens at Meyer's headquarters in nearby Ardenne. Twenty-three of them never came out alive.

Later, in the square at Authie, guffawing SS troops propped a dead Canadian against the wall of a house, put a German helmet on his head, a cigarette in his mouth, and a beer bottle in the crook of his arm.

On another occasion, a German staff car raced by, horn klaxoning, while a soldier in the back seat took pot shots at prisoners. Two Canadians staggered, hit in the stomach, much to the amusement of their German guards. Another prisoner whispered something to a friend, and as the man turned to answer, an SS guard emptied the slugs from a submachine gun into his stomach.

German vehicles began speeding both ways around the Authie square, some loaded with German wounded who shook their fists at the Canadian prisoners. A big truck deliberately swerved into marching prisoners and two of the captives died on the pavement. A guard said to a nearby Canadian who was shocked at the brutal slaying of his comrades: "You bombed Germany. Can you expect mercy?"

On June 8, at a 12th SS Command Post, six members of

The Royal Winnipeg Rifles were ordered into the woods and shot. One was a stretcher-bearer wearing the armband of the Red Cross. Later that same day, 13 more Winnipegs were shot just outside the command post. The bodies of seven others were found nearby, without weapons or equipment. All had been killed by small arms fire.

**Shoot The Wounded**
That evening, 40 Winnipegs and Cameron Highlanders were marched into a field and ordered to sit close together, with the wounded in the centre. German soldiers opened fire and 35 Canadians toppled over dead. When the shooting started, five other prisoners darted for a nearby wheat field and escaped — but not before witnessing the slaughter of their comrades.

Two Regina Rifles were captured on outpost duty on June 9 and questioned by a German officer. When he didn't like the answers he was given, he pulled out his Luger pistol and shot them. One soldier was killed instantly. The other pretended to be dead and eventually got back to his battalion — another witness to the barbarian slaughter. That same morning, three wounded Canadians were forced to march into a garden and were shot by four German soldiers.

There were reports of the bodies of murdered Canadian prisoners being dragged into the middle of a road, where convoys of German trucks and tanks rumbled over them. Other indignities to the bodies of dead prisoners were also reported, but they are too gruesome to be recounted here.

It didn't take long for stories about the German atrocities to get back to Canadian and British troops in the area, and the story goes that German soldiers attempting to surrender were shot and killed.

While perhaps understandable, these acts of revenge were regrettable — not only because they reduced Allied soldiers to the same level as the fiendish SS and Hitler Jugend, but because they later proved to be a blessing in disguise for the murderous Kurt Meyer.

# Chapter 7
# The Bitter Battle For Caen

eneral Montgomery and his military strategists had allowed their optimism to get the better of them in believing that the D-Day troops could establish a beachhead on the Normandy coast and — on the very same day — push inland through fierce German resistance to capture the heavily defended city of Caen.

Just how naïve the military strategists were can be illustrated by the fact that many of the soldiers in the second wave of Canadian assault troops were issued bicycles for what was expected to be an easy romp inland. Needless to say, dozens of the two-wheelers were dumped in the shallows of Juno Beach as the troops scrambled toward dry land under withering enemy fire.

Canadian troops, most of whom just days before had never seen anything bloodier in their lives than a broken nose in a high school hockey or football game, were expected to perform military miracles. They had to land under withering fire, witness their friends being cut to ribbons, rout the battle-hardened Nazis from concrete bunkers, then advance 12 to 15 kilometres inland to lend support to equally battle weary British troops whose orders were to take Caen that very day.

It would, in fact, take a month to achieve that objective — and the Canadians would be among the first Allied troops to enter the centuries-old capital city of the Calvados region.

Three battalions of the 716th German Infantry Division defended the Normandy coast, and other divisions were close by. But what even Montgomery and his advisors were unaware of, due to a gap in intelligence reports, was that the real enemy strength lay in the 21st Panzer Division near Caen. Another wild card was the fanatical 12th SS Division containing the battle-hardened veterans of the Russian Front and Führer-worshipping Hitler Youth.

**Out Of Action**
After six days of bloody battles that included 1017 dead, 1814 wounded, and many others suffering battle fatigue, the 3rd Canadian Infantry Division was pulled out of action for two weeks to rest up, refill their decimated ranks, and prepare to

take up the fight once again.

When they were sent back into action early in July, the Canadians were ordered again to capture the airport at Carpiquet, held by about 150 of the now-experienced and even more fanatical Hitler Jugend. They were under the command of a recently promoted Brigadeführer (Major General) Kurt Meyer.

The capture of Carpiquet airfield was assigned to The North Shore Regiment, The Queen's Own, the Chaudières, and The Royal Winnipeg Rifles. The Canadians were aware that the Germans had the advantage of well-built underground blockhouses with connecting passageways. What they didn't know was that German radio operators also had possession of a Canadian codebook.

To try to oust the Germans from their subterranean bunkers, the Canadians requested a pre-attack artillery barrage on the morning of July 4 that included 428 field guns, backed up by the firepower of warships lying off the Normandy coast. The Canadians then attacked with tanks and flamethrowers, and met with fierce resistance. While the town and part of the airfield were captured, the two sides fought to a standstill that lasted until the attack on Caen. Canadian casualties were high, with 117 dead and 260 wounded or captured.

**On To Caen**

On the night of July 7, the Allies in the Caen area were treated

Infantry men with a Bren gun looking out for snipers
on a street corner, Caen, July 1944

to a morale-boosting display of RAF carpet bombing to soften up the enemy within the city of 55,000 inhabitants. Some 467 bombers unloaded more than 2500 tons of explosives on the city as the Allies stood on the high ground nearby and cheered like schoolboys. Their cheers would have caught in their throats if they had realized that most of the Germans had already left Caen and it was mainly civilians who would be counted among the 400 dead and thousands wounded.

The Canadians would once again engage in the bloodiest fighting in the small villages on the outer perimeter of Caen. Old names and old battles came back to haunt them. They found themselves once again pitted against their ubiquitous nemeses, Kurt Meyer and the 12th SS, in places like Buron and Authie.

Fresh troops of The Highland Light Infantry suffered a gruesome baptism under fire at Buron, where an all-day battle left them with a loss of more than 250 men, including their commanding officer.

But The North Nova Scotia Highlanders captured Authie, and The Regina Rifles and Sherbrooke Fusiliers battled the Nazi troops long past nightfall, the battleground lit up dramatically by the flaming torches of Canadian and German tanks.

An eerie calm descended over the area the next morning. Meyer and his troops had disappeared, using the cloak of darkness to scramble over the River Orne to fight another day. There were still fierce battles ahead as the Canadian and British troops slowly pushed their way into the city. The bombing and shelling had left mounds of rubble, which provided ample cover for German snipers as well as mines and booby traps.

The Stormont, Dundas and Glengarry Highlanders,

along with the tanks of the Sherbrooke Fusiliers, were the first Canadians into Caen. To their amazement, the famous 1000-year-old L'Abbaye-aux-Hommes rose out of the surrounding rubble unscathed. Not a bomb or shell had touched it.

Inside the cathedral were 2000 people who had lived there for several weeks. Despite the fact that their beloved city lay in ruins, with two-thirds of the original buildings and ancient monuments having been destroyed by Allied bombardment, the citizens welcomed the liberating troops with open arms.

It had cost the Canadians dearly to play a decisive role in the capture of Caen. Casualties included 330 dead and 864 wounded — more than the Canadian toll on D-Day. And there would be many more battles and much more bloodshed before Hitler and his Third Reich were defeated. But many Canadian veterans speak of the prolonged battle to capture Caen the way their counterparts in World War I talked of Vimy Ridge — a proud symbol of the tenacity and fighting spirit of the Canadian soldier in the face of overwhelming odds.

# Chapter 8
# The End Of
# The Beginning

After the British victory over General Rommel in North Africa, Great Britain's Prime Minister, Winston Churchill, commented: "Now this is not the end. It is not even the beginning of the end. But it is, perhaps, the end of the beginning."

From a Canadian perspective, he could well have been speaking about the situation after the Battle of Caen. Ask the average Canadian today when World War II ended and the most common answer will probably be: "On D-Day when the Americans, British, and Canadians landed in Northern France."

But D-Day certainly wasn't the end. As of June 6, 1944, there was still an 11-month campaign of brutal and bloody fighting ahead. And those thousands of Canadian D-Day troops who were yet to lose their lives in countless battles in France, Belgium, Holland, and Germany would be unlikely to consider it the beginning of the end. Yet, in retrospect, it would seem safe to say that it was definitely the end of the beginning.

After the taking of Caen, the battle-weary Canadians received reinforcements when the 2nd Canadian Infantry Division reached France under the command of Major General Charles Foulkes. Together with the units already in Normandy, they formed the 2nd Canadian Corps under the command of Lieutenant General Guy G. Simonds.

On July 19, after fierce hand-to-hand combat in the bombed-out rubble of the industrial suburbs of Caen, the 2nd Canadian Corps, along with the 7th British Armoured and Guards Armoured Divisions, managed to cross the Orne River — not without heavy losses, however. On July 20, the Canadian 2nd Division set out along with several British units to capture Verrières Ridge, a tactically important high point controlling access to the road running south from Caen. The ridge was defended by the 1st Leibstandarte Adolf Hitler, an experienced SS unit that was fresh from destroying one of the British Army's crack units.

The battle for the ridge turned into a slaughter of Allied troops, who failed to take their objective. When the smoke had cleared, the Germans still controlled the ridge and various units of the Canadian attack force were decimated. The

2nd Canadian Corps had lost almost 2000 men in the four days of fighting.

The Corps got another chance to take the ridge on July 25, but once again they were repulsed by the more experienced Germans. By the time this second assault was called off, the operation had produced more than 1500 casualties, about 450 of them fatalities. Other than the tragedy of Dieppe, this would go down in military history as the most devastating day of the war for the Canadians.

**The Falaise Gap**
On August 14, after a week or more of heavy losses, the Canadians launched Operation Tractable, a major offensive to meet with American forces advancing from the south and seal off the Germans at Falaise. Joined by the 2nd Canadian Division, General Simonds and his troops took Falaise on August 17. With the Americans and troops of the Polish Armoured Division linking up at Chambois on August 20 and being joined by the tanks of the 4th Canadian Armoured Division's Grenadier Guards the next day, the Germans were trapped in the pocket while Allied air forces pounded their positions.

Another Canadian was awarded the Victoria Cross during this stage of the Normandy battle. The recipient was The South Alberta Regiment's Major David Vivian Currie of Sutherland, Saskatchewan, for his heroic action on August 18.

Major Currie was in command of a small mixed force of Canadian tanks, self-propelled anti-tank guns, and infantry troops ordered to cut one of the main escape routes from the Falaise pocket. The force was held up by strong enemy resistance in the village of St. Lambert-sur-Dives, and two tanks were knocked out. Major Currie immediately entered the village alone on foot through enemy outposts to reconnoitre the German defences and successfully extricate the crews from the disabled tanks under a deadly mortar barrage by Nazi troops.

Early the following morning, Major Currie led an attack on the village under heavy fire, and set up a defensive position. During the next 36 hours, he and his men withstood one counterattack after another, eventually destroying 7 enemy tanks, 12 88mm guns, and 40 vehicles, while killing 300 Germans, wounding 500, and capturing 2100.

Although thousands of Germans were able to slip out of the Falaise trap, virtually no tanks or vehicles survived. The Allies were successful in capturing almost half of the Wehrmacht and equipment then in Normandy. The Germans were finally on the run.

**Dieppe Revenge**
Dieppe resident Jacques Dubost would recall after the war that on the blood-soaked day of August 19, 1942, a Canadian soldier, in a futile attempt to escape capture by the victorious Germans, appeared in the garden adjacent to the Dubost

home and shouted: "We'll be back." Then he headed for the beach where the scattered bodies of Canadian soldiers lay in the awkward splay of violent death.

It took two years, one week, and six days, but on September 1, 1944, the Canadians did come back. And so did war correspondent Ross Munro, who had witnessed the carnage of the earlier raid, and whose war coverage would see him awarded the rank of Officer in the Order of the British Empire (OBE). In *Gauntlet to Overlord*, the Canadian Press reporter recounted that triumphant return less than two weeks after the Allies' stunning victory in Normandy:

"After several days of heavy fighting in the Forêt de la Londe, the Canadians rolled into Rouen. From morning to night on the last day of August, convoys of the 2nd Division whisked through the city. Columns of carriers and half-tracks, tanks and guns and hundreds of trucks filled with fighting men passed down the wide thoroughfares lined with ecstatic French people offering a wild, prolonged welcome. But the 2nd Division could not tarry. It had a rendezvous with history 40 miles (64 kilometres) away.

"On the outskirts of Rouen, the highway forks — left to Le Havre, right to Dieppe. A crowd watched the Canadians wheel to the right. '*Ca, c'est bien!*' they shouted. '*Les Canadiens s'en vont à Dieppe.*' (That's wonderful. The Canadians are going to Dieppe.)

"The columns sped north up the long, straight road. Leading was the 8th Reconnaissance Regiment, with one of its squadrons under Major Dennis Bult-Francis of Montreal, who had been wounded in the 1942 raid. Behind came the Dieppe regiments — The Essex Scottish, The Royal Regiment of Canada, The Royal Hamilton Light Infantry, The South Saskatchewans and others. There were about 25 survivors of the raid in each infantry battalion. Neither they nor the men who had replaced the casualties of 1942 thought Dieppe would be taken without a battle. The units had been briefed for assault. Bomber Command was to raid the port in the early evening of September 1st. Warships were to shell coastal positions. The plan called for a large-scale combined operation.

"At Tôtes, halfway to Dieppe, there was a sharp brush with a German anti-aircraft unit withdrawing from Le Havre peninsula; there was another at Longueville. By nightfall, the 8th Recce was just short of Dieppe; the rest of the division was stretched out for a dozen miles (20 kilometres) behind them.

"At 10:30 a.m. on September 1st, they entered Dieppe. The Germans had gone, had fled even as they approached. Instead of bullets and blood, Dieppe gave the Canadians flowers and wine. A delirious population poured into the streets to shout that the town was free."

**Antwerp And The Scheldt**
British and Canadian troops continued their sweep across northern France, with Boulogne and Calais being liberated

shortly after Dieppe. The rapid advance, however, meant that the Allies were running short of supplies. Fierce storms off the Normandy Coast had destroyed one Mulberry Harbour and badly damaged the second.

Since there weren't enough other ports in Allied hands to compensate for the loss of the artificial harbours, the Canadians were ordered to cross the Belgian border and capture the massive port facilities at Antwerp. The facilities were taken virtually intact, but the military strategists had overlooked one small problem — the Germans still controlled the Scheldt Estuary, the long and winding stretch of river channels and islands leading from the sea to Antwerp, a distance of about 80 kilometres.

Allied shipping would be blown out of the water as long as the Nazis were in control of the estuary. It would have to be cleared of an enemy that was well dug in. Part of their defences included Walcheren Island, fortified into a German stronghold. The south bank of the estuary — flat, low-lying land reclaimed from the sea — was below sea level and also well suited to defence. Nevertheless, Antwerp Harbour was useless without control of the sea access and something would have to be done about it.

The job fell to the First Canadian Army, which came under the command of General Simonds, who replaced an ailing General Crerar. Armour was virtually useless in an area capillaried with canals. The infantry had to inch forward under heavy enemy fire through sand, mud, and water. In fact, those who faced this onerous task came to be known as the "Water Rats."

One of the casualties of the Scheldt offensive would go on to greater things after the war. Major (acting) H. Clifford Chadderton of Fort William (now Thunder Bay), Ontario was with The Royal Winnipeg Rifles and had risen from the ranks of non-commissioned officer to company commander.

Major Chadderton was wounded twice, once by a bullet at the Abbaye d'Ardenne — the infamous headquarters of SS Major General Kurt Meyer — and a second time by a grenade near the Leopold Canal during the Scheldt offensive, where he lost his right leg below the knee. Major Chadderton's devotion to duty outlasted the war. As Chief Executive Officer of the War Amputations of Canada and Chairman of the National Council of Veteran Associations in Canada, he took on the role of championing the cause of veterans and amputees, many of the latter being children.

In five weeks of hard going, the Canadians suffered more than 6000 casualties, but the battle was won. The jubilant and normally taciturn Field Marshal Montgomery was moved to say: "The Canadians have proved themselves magnificent fighters. Clearing the Scheldt was a job that could have been done only by first-rate troops. Second-rate troops would have failed."

Not to be outdone, Montgomery's superior officer, General Eisenhower, upon hearing that the first Allied ship — fittingly enough the Canadian-built *Fort Cataraqui* — had brought its cargo up the estuary to dock at Antwerp, also had high praise. "The end of Nazism was in clear view when the first ship moved unmolested up the Scheldt." From that point on, a steady stream of supplies and war materiel poured into Antwerp, opening the way for the final Allied assault on Germany itself.

**The Rhineland Campaign**

After their success in the Scheldt Estuary, the Canadians were ordered to hold the line along the Maas and the Nijmegen Salient. This was largely a standoff exercise to give the Allies time to plan a major advance in the spring — designed to push the enemy back over the Rhine River and bring about total surrender.

On February 8, 1945, Operation Veritable began, preceded by a devastating air and artillery attack on enemy concentrations. The objective was for British, Canadian, and American forces to clear the great Reichwald Forest, break through the infamous Siegfried Line, overrun the Hochwald Forest defences, and close up units at the Rhine.

Progress was slow. Mud and flooded ground bogged down the troops, who at times had to slog through water three feet deep. Nevertheless, the outer defences of the Siegfried Line fell and the Water Rats of the 3rd Canadian Infantry Division, adept at amphibious manoeuvres after their successes in the Scheldt, made significant gains.

On February 21, the British and Canadian troops

cracked the Siegfried Line and, after a bloody battle, captured Hochwald. The Americans were progressing from the south against heavy resistance. On March 10, the Germans detonated the bridges at Wesel and withdrew to the east bank of the Rhine.

In a month of doing battle, Canadian losses amounted to 5304 killed, wounded, or missing in action, but they had reached the banks of the Rhine, considered the last major line of German defence.

**The Final Push**

The time had come for the final phase of the campaign in Northwest Europe. On March 23, Field Marshal Montgomery's Allied forces commenced the attack across the Rhine. The troops of the 9th Canadian Infantry Brigade, under British command, took part in the crossing at Rees. The 1st Parachute Battalion, as part of the British 6th Airborne Division, made a successful jump east of the Rhine near Wesel. Several days later, the 3rd Division crossed the Rhine and battled as far as Emmerich.

In the final months of the war, the Canadian Army's mandate was to open up the supply route to the north through Arnhem, then take out German defences in the northeastern Netherlands, clear the German coastal area eastward to the Elbe River, and occupy western Holland.

At this point, the 1st Canadian Corps transferred to Northwest Europe from their bloody push through Italy to bolster the First Canadian Army. For the first time in history, two Canadian Army Corps would fight side by side, pushing rapidly north and playing a significant role in kicking the Nazis out of the Netherlands.

While the troops of the 2nd Canadian Corps were being hailed as liberators in northeastern Holland, the 1st Canadian Corps was clearing out the area north of the Maas River. The populous cities of Amsterdam, Rotterdam, and The Hague were on the brink of starvation after what would go down in history as the "Hunger Winter." Children carried spoons with them to scrape the last edible scraps out of garbage cans.

By April 28, the Germans in West Holland had been backed up to a line stretching approximately from Wageningen through Amersfoort to the sea. This was known as the Grebbe Line. Immediately, the Allies arranged a temporary truce with the Germans — threatening their officers with war crime charges if they refused — in order to allow the movement of food and fuel supplies to the starving, half-frozen Dutch people.

At the same time that the Canadians were enjoying the role of liberators of Holland, Germany's Third Reich was on the verge of collapse. With the Russians over-running Berlin, Adolf Hitler married his long-time mistress, Eva Braun, in a bunker under the besieged German capital. They then committed suicide and their bodies were burned by the few loyal followers who had stayed with Der Führer to the bitter end.

Karl Dönitz, Grand Admiral of the Germany Navy, assumed command of what was left of the German military forces.

On May 5, in the village of Wageningen, General Foulkes accepted the surrender of the German troops in Holland. General Simonds did the same on his front, in the German seaside resort town of Bad Zwischenahn.

The formal surrender was signed on May 7 in the French city of Reims. Canada had been at war for almost six years. It was time for the men — and the women who had served in various support roles — to go home.

# Chapter 9
# Getting Away With Murder

One of the gruesome yet necessary clean-up jobs after a war is the prosecution of alleged war criminals and their execution if they are found guilty of crimes against humanity. One such trial involved the butcher of Normandy, SS Brigadeführer Kurt Meyer.

Meyer had been captured by the Americans in Belgium in September 1944 but, unlike the proud SS officer he claimed to be, he hid his identity for a month by wearing a Wehrmacht uniform. Once the Americans realized Meyer was an officer of the murderous SS, he was sent to England for interrogation and incarcerated as a prisoner of war while deliberations as to what should be done with him took place amongst the Allied powers.

At this point, stories began to emerge about the atrocities committed by Meyer's 12th SS Panzer Division against Canadian prisoners during the Normandy campaign. These stories were related by embittered Canadian veterans, French witnesses, and former SS members seeking to save their own skin. Meyer was subsequently put on trial before a Canadian Military Court in Aurich, Germany, on December 10, 1945.

The prosecutor was Lieutenant Colonel Bruce Macdonald of The Essex Scottish Regiment. (Assisting Lieutenant Colonel Macdonald at the trial was Lieutenant Colonel Clarence Campbell, who would find himself in another emotion-charged situation 10 years later when, as President of the National Hockey League, he tangled with Montreal hockey fans by suspending their beloved Maurice "Rocket" Richard.)

The court was convened by Major General Chris Vokes, the general officer commanding the Canadian occupation forces. Lieutenant Colonel Macdonald revealed that investigations had established that atrocities were committed in 31 different incidents involving 134 Canadians, three British, and one American.

Meyer brought into the courtroom with him a reputation for being a brave soldier and brilliant tactician. But also swirling around him were tales of his burning down villages and murdering women, children, and Russian soldiers during his time on the Eastern Front before he was sent to Normandy as Commander of the 25th Panzer Grenadier Regiment of the 12th SS Panzer Division.

## Quarter Denied

As journalist Charmion Chaplin-Thomas reported from the little northern German town of Aurich on the day the trail commenced, Meyer stood accused of inciting his troops to "deny quarter" — that is, kill prisoners. He was being held personally accountable for the murder of 27 Canadian prisoners of war by troops under his command.

Charmion-Chaplin pointed out that Meyer's troops had in fact murdered at least 156 captured soldiers of The 3rd Canadian Infantry Division. However, only the deaths of 27 members of The North Nova Scotia Highlanders, Les Fusiliers de Sherbrooke, The Royal Winnipeg Rifles, and The Queen's Own Rifles of Canada were under discussion because only they could be directly connected to Meyer by witnesses.

One of the witnesses for the prosecution was Jan Jesionek, a Polish conscript who said he heard Meyer instruct his officers not to take prisoners. Another witness was Daniel Lachèvre, a 15-year-old boy who lived at L'Abbaye d'Ardenne. The Abbaye was the site of two massacres in which 18 prisoners died. Daniel testified that Meyer lied about the events, casting blame for the prisoners' deaths on a subordinate.

Meyer, not surprisingly, pleaded not guilty to all charges. In total, 29 witnesses were called and Meyer eventually took the stand in his own defence. On December 28,

Meyer was found guilty of the charges of inciting and coun-
selling his men to deny quarter to Allied troops. He was also
held responsible for the shootings at his headquarters at the
Abbaye, but not guilty of ordering them. He was found not to
be responsible for shootings outside his headquarters.

The president of the court, Major General Harry Foster,
sentenced Meyer to death. Amidst howls of protest from
Canadian veterans, from families of the martyred prisoners
of war, and from Canadians in general, this sentence was
later commuted to life imprisonment.

The commutation decision was bizarre, to say the least.
As was his right, Meyer appealed for clemency to the conven-
ing officer of the court, Major General Vokes, on January 5,
1945. Vokes denied the appeal, stating, "I have considered
this appeal and cannot see my way clear to mitigate the punishment awarded by the Court."

**Officer Reverses Himself**
This "firm" decision was followed by a ludicrous turn of
events in which the major general, wearing another hat,
actually overruled himself — and he did so under an escape
clause that had been entered into the trial procedures manu-
al by none other than the Canadian prosecutor, Lieutenant
Colonel Macdonald.

In his efforts to be scrupulously fair, Lieutenant Colonel
Macdonald, having a major role in drawing up the military
tribunal regulations, had included what amounted to a

"notwithstanding" clause. This section stated that a convicted war criminal should have the right of a final appeal to someone not connected to the trial itself, namely the senior commanding officer in the theatre. Section 14 of the regulations stated that this officer "shall have the power to mitigate or remit the punishment thereby awarded, or to commute such punishment for any lesser punishment."

Lieutenant Colonel Macdonald, apparently concerned that justice not only be done, but also, as Lord Hewart once pointed out, "should manifestly and undoubtedly be seen to be done," brought the matter up himself a few days after clemency had been rejected. Nobody had thought to invoke this regulation, but a review was hastily arranged.

In one of the weirdest twists of jurisprudence, the realization struck home that the senior commanding officer was, in fact, Major General Vokes, the same officer who had already rejected Meyer's appeal for clemency.

Nevertheless, Vokes, on this occasion, perversely ruled in favour of commutation, suggesting that the severity of the sentence was not in keeping with Canadian justice, "having regard to the degree of responsibility for the killings."

Military historians believe that Major General Vokes actually made this decision because he was aware that Canadian and British troops had also "taken no prisoners" once the stories of German atrocities began to circulate on the battlefields of Normandy.

At any rate, Meyer strutted out of the courtroom and

into a cell in New Brunswick's Dorchester Penitentiary to serve out his life sentence. But he still wasn't through thumbing his nose at Canada's justice system. Transferred to Werl, a prison for Nazi war criminals in the British Zone of Germany, Meyer proceeded to get influential German and British pre-war colleagues to bring pressure against the Canadian government to get him released. On January 15, 1954, the life sentence was commuted, and later that year, Meyer walked away from prison a free man.

He spent the rest of his life selling beer — and making speeches to German veterans' groups about the glories of The Third Reich. He died, apparently with a clear conscience, on December 23, 1961.

# *Appendix A*
# Allied Military Leaders

### General Dwight David Eisenhower
Born: Denison, Texas, October 14, 1890
Died: Washington, DC, March 28, 1969

Born in Texas, Dwight Eisenhower grew up in Abilene, Kansas. Between 1911 and 1915, he attended the West Point Military Academy. He was not able to take part in actual military action during World War I, having been assigned training duties.

He followed courses at the Command and General Staff School in Leavenworth, Kansas, in 1925, and later at the Army Staff College in Washington, DC, from which he graduated in 1928. He served in several general staff positions during the years before the U.S. involvement in World War II.

In 1940–41, he was Executive Officer with the 15th Infantry Regiment, then Chief of Staff, 3rd Division, and finally, Chief of Staff, 3rd Army. In 1942, the Army's Chief of

Staff, George Marshal, was looking for new faces for operational command postings. In March, he appointed Eisenhower as Chief of Operations Division, and two months later sent him to London as Commander of U.S. forces in Europe.

In 1942, Eisenhower took part in the discussions of the Combined Chiefs of Staff to determine how best to attack Germany, and he was given the command of Operation Torch, the Invasion of North Africa, which started on November 8, 1942.

In July 1943, Eisenhower led the invasion of Sicily. The ground forces involved in that operation included the U.S. 7th Army and the British 8th Army, under General Bernard Montgomery. The 1st Canadian Infantry Division was part of the 8th Army.

Eisenhower then took command of the joint ground forces that landed in continental Italy on September 8, 1943. He was not to lead that campaign to its conclusion, however, being recalled to London in December to take over the Supreme Command of the forces that prepared the invasion of France.

As Commander of SHEAF (Supreme Headquarters, Allied Expeditionary Force), Eisenhower had to combine Allied armies, navies, and air forces to build the largest invading force ever assembled. To assist him, he had a general staff of some 16,000 men and officers.

After the armistice was signed on May 8, 1945,

## Appendix A

Eisenhower commanded the Occupation Forces for six months. He then succeeded George Marshal as Chief of Staff of the U.S. Army, a position he held until 1948. From April 2, 1951 to May 30, 1952, Eisenhower was SACEUR (Supreme Allied Commander, Europe).

He left the military to run in the U.S. presidential elections. An immensely popular war hero, he won an easy victory and was inaugurated on January 20, 1953. He won a second term in 1956.

### Field Marshal Bernard Montgomery
Born: London, England, November 17, 1887
Died: Alton, Hampshire, March 24, 1976

Bernard Montgomery was the son of an Anglican bishop. He attended St. Paul's School and the Sandhurst Military Academy. In 1908, he enlisted with the Royal Warwickshire Regiment. He served in India for some time, and after World War I broke out, he served in France, where he was severely wounded.

Montgomery was back on the front in 1916 and, after the war, served as Chief of General Staff for the 47th London Division. Already he was regarded as a remarkable officer for training the troops, an officer who believed that top physical fitness went hand in hand with good leadership.

During the early months of World War II, Montgomery commanded the 2nd Army Corps. Unable to stop the progression of German troops, he was forced to retreat towards Dunkirk, and from there, to sail back to England on June 1, 1940.

In August 1942, Winston Churchill put Montgomery in command of the 8th Army, which had just been defeated by Erwin Rommel's Afrika Korps. Montgomery was able to rebuild the morale of his troops. The 8th Army, advancing cautiously, drove back the Germans and forced them to regroup outside Egypt after a decisive battle at El Alamein in November 1942. It was the first Allied victory against Nazi Germany — a victory that gave the British some confidence and confirmed "Monty's" reputation.

On September 3, 1943, he led the 8th Army, landing in Reggio di Calabria in southern Italy and then proceeding northward. At that time, Montgomery had under his command the 5th and 10th British Corps, the 2nd Polish Corps, and the 1st Canadian Corps under Lieutenant General H.D.G. Crerar.

In December 1943, Monty was called back to England to take command of the land forces for the Invasion of Normandy. He was Commander-in-Chief, 21st Army Group during the campaign in northwestern Europe, which started with D-Day and lasted until the final surrender of Germany.

When the war ended, Montgomery had been a Field Marshal since September 1, 1944. In 1946, he was made a Knight of the Garter and 1st Viscount Montgomery of Alamein to salute his outstanding contribution to the Allied victory.

# Appendix A

## General Andrew G.L. McNaughton

Born: Moosomin, Northwest Territories
(now Saskatchewan), February 25, 1887
Died: Montebello, Quebec, July 11, 1966

Andrew McNaughton graduated in physics and engineering from McGill University in Montreal. He enlisted in the militia in 1909, then, in 1914, in the 4th Battery of the Canadian Expeditionary Corps. Applying his scientific knowledge to artillery, he was rapidly promoted, and when World War I ended, he was head of the Canadian Artillery Corps.

After World War I, McNaughton remained with the Canadian Permanent Forces as Chief of the General Staff. He worked at mechanizing the armed forces and modernizing the militia. Returning to civilian life in 1935, he was head of the National Research Council of Canada.

With the outbreak of World War II, McNaughton became Commanding Officer of the 1st Canadian Infantry Division. Under his leadership, the division grew and was reorganized as a corps in 1940 and then as an army in 1942.

McNaughton unfortunately ran afoul of General Montgomery, who wanted to use the troops supplied by the "Dominion" as if they were British units, dividing them up when the need arose. McNaughton dug in his heels in opposition to this return to a colonial attitude by Great Britain. Criticized for his stance and weakened by health problems, McNaughton resigned his command in December 1943.

He was appointed Minister of Defence by Prime Minister Mackenzie King in 1944, but once again he landed into a controversy — this time over the unpopular matter of conscription. He failed to gain the support of Canadian voters, and was not elected to the House of Commons.

After the war, he served on several commissions and was Permanent Representative to the United Nations in 1948–49. Between 1950 and 1959, he served as President of the Canadian section of the International Joint Commission.

### General H.D.G. Crerar
Born: Hamilton, Ontario, April 28, 1888
Died: Ottawa, Ontario, April 1, 1965

Harry Crerar was educated at the Royal Military College in Kingston, Ontario, from 1906 to 1909, and joined the militia in the years preceding World War I. During the war, he served with distinction as a Canadian Field Artillery officer on French and Flanders battlefields, and was awarded the Distinguished Service Order. At the cessation of hostilities, he was a Lieutenant Colonel on the Canadian Corps' General Staff.

Back in Canada, Crerar opted for a military career and joined the Permanent Force as Staff Officer Artillery in Ottawa. In 1923, he matriculated at the Camberley Staff College in England, and accepted a posting as General Staff Officer 2 with the War Office in London. In 1929, Crerar was

## Appendix A

appointed General Staff Officer 1 at National Defence Headquarters (NDHQ) in Ottawa. He started working on a major reorganization of the Canadian Militia.

In 1934, Crerar was once again in England, following courses at the Imperial Defence College in London. Back to NDHQ, he became Director of Military Operations and Intelligence. He was perceived as the best officer on the Canadian General Staff. In March 1939, after serving a few months as Commander of the Royal Military College, Crerar was recalled to Ottawa to prepare a mobilization plan as the possibility of another war increased.

As World War II began, Crerar was posted to London as Brigadier General at the Canadian Military HQ, and was responsible for ensuring that the required equipment, barracks, and training plans were in place when Canadian troops arrived. In July 1940, he was recalled to Ottawa and promoted to Chief of the General Staff. He took immediate measures to improve the efficiency of NDHQ, and set up emergency recruitment and training programs for territorial defence as well as a training program for officers and soldiers slated to serve overseas.

Crerar returned to England where, on December 23, 1941, he was appointed General Officer Commanding, 1st Canadian Corps, serving with the unit in Italy from October 1943 until he was recalled to England in March 1944 to take over the command of the First Canadian Army, replacing General McNaughton.

# D-Day

The First Canadian Army was mustered in Normandy on July 23, 1944, and, under Crerar's command, it played a major role as the Allies circled German troops in the Falaise Gap in August 1944. Ill health forced Crerar to be replaced temporarily by Major General Guy Simonds during the Battle of the Scheldt in October–November 1944. In February 1945, the First Canadian Army, with Crerar back at the helm, was once more on the front line. During the Rhineland Campaign, he found himself at the head of a 450,000-man army, including Allied units under First Canadian Army command.

Crerar retired from the military in 1946. Later, he occupied diplomatic postings in Czechoslovakia, the Netherlands, and Japan.

### Lieutenant General Guy Simonds
Born: Bury St. Edmunds, England, April 23, 1903
Died: Toronto, Ontario, May 15, 1974

The son of a British officer who immigrated to Canada, Guy Simonds was too young to serve in World War I. Between 1921 and 1925, he studied at the Royal Military College in Kingston, Ontario, graduating with honours. He received several awards for his academic success, his behaviour, and his discipline.

Simonds joined the Canadian Permanent Force in 1926, serving with The Royal Canadian Horse Artillery in Petawawa, Ontario, and Winnipeg, Manitoba. Between 1936

## Appendix A

and 1938, the young captain furthered his education at the Staff College in Camberley, England, receiving a laudatory recommendation from the college's commanding officer upon graduation.

Back in Canada, Simonds joined the staff of the Royal Military College. Upon proclamation of war on September 10, 1939, Simonds, then a major, was appointed as General Staff Officer Grade 2 with the 1st Infantry Division. He took his division to England in December 1939.

In July 1940, Simonds was posted with the 1st Field Regiment of the Royal Canadian Artillery, then chosen by General Andrew McNaughton to set up the Canadian Junior War Staff Course, an intensive training program for officers.

Highly regarded for his remarkable military and planning skills, Simonds rose through the military hierarchy very quickly — General Staff Officer, Grade 1, with the 2nd Infantry Division in May 1941; Commander of the 1st Infantry Brigade in September 1942; and then Major General, Commander of the 1st Canadian Infantry Division in April 1943.

Simonds' first combat experience took place with the invasion of Sicily, where he commanded the 1st Infantry Division and came to the attention of General Bernard Montgomery. From November 1, 1943, to January 29, 1944, Simonds led the 5th Canadian Armoured Division. He was promoted to Lieutenant General at this point, and General Officer Commanding of the 2nd Canadian Corps in preparation for D-Day.

The 2nd Canadian Corps set up its headquarters in Normandy in July 1944. In July and August, Simonds headed four very important engagements against German positions. These were difficult operations against an enemy desperately fighting for each square inch of a terrain with which it was familiar. During Operation Totalize on August 7, Simonds invented the "Kangaroo," an improvised troop carrier made by taking the guns off a "Priest" self-propelled gun. On August 14, Operation Tractable allowed Canadian and Polish troops to close the Falaise Gap.

On September 27, 1944, Simonds took charge of the First Canadian Army on a temporary basis, replacing an ailing General Crerar, and headed the operation that liberated the mouth of the Scheldt River, thus opening up Antwerp Harbour to Allied shipping. Upon Crerar's return, Simonds resumed command of the 2nd Canadian Corps for the liberation of Northwestern Europe.

After the war, Simonds remained in England with the Imperial Defence College. He returned to Canada as Commander of the Kingston Royal Military College in 1949. Between 1951 and 1955, he served as Chief of the General Staff, reorganizing the Canadian Army in preparation for the Korean War, and later, for NATO operations.

### Lieutenant General Charles Foulkes

Born: Stockton-on-Tees, England, January 3, 1903
Died: Ottawa, Ontario, September 12, 1969

## Appendix A

After a few years of university education, Charles Foulkes joined the Canadian Permanent Force in 1926. He then became a general staff officer with The Royal Canadian Regiment before attending Staff College in Camberley, England, in 1937.

When World War II broke out, Foulkes was a major with the 3rd Brigade of the 1st Canadian Infantry Division. In September 1940, he was appointed General Staff Officer Grade 1 with the 3rd Canadian Infantry Division, becoming Brigadier Commander in August 1942. In August 1943, Foulkes became Brigadier, General Staff, with the First Canadian Army.

In January 1944, he replaced Major General E.L.M Burns as General Officer Commanding the 2nd Infantry Division, a unit that he headed up during the Normandy Campaign. In November 1944, Foulkes joined the 1st Canadian Corps, then serving in Italy, as General Officer Commanding. He remained the commanding officer of the corps until the end of the Italy Campaign, and later through the liberation of the Netherlands.

Foulkes accepted the surrender of the German forces in Wageningen, Netherlands, on May 5, 1945. After the war, he was appointed Chief of General Staff and, in 1951, Chairman of the Chiefs of Staff Committee. He retired in 1960.

(Courtesy: Defence Canada)

# *Appendix B*
# Glossary of Military Terms

**Army** – Two or more corps under the command of a general; generally between 120,000 and 200,000 all ranks.

**Army Group** – Two or more armies under the command of a field marshal; generally between 400,000 and one million all ranks. The largest land force formation.

**Battalion** – The basic combat unit of the Army. A Canadian infantry battalion included four rifle companies and a support company, which was equipped with heavier weapons. The total strength was about 850 personnel.

**Battery** – A company-sized sub-unit of artillery, whose major equipment was usually eight artillery pieces. The most common artillery weapon was the 25-pounder, which fired an explosive 11-kilogram shell to a range of about 10 kilometres. Two or more batteries made up an artillery regiment.

**Beachhead** – The landing site on enemy territory after having crossed a large expanse of water.

**Brigade** – An army formation of two or more battalions (or regiments in the case of armoured brigades) of up to 5000 men. The Canadian Army had both infantry and armoured (i.e. tank) brigades.

**Company** – A body of about 100 soldiers, commanded by a major or captain. There are four companies to a battalion. Although basically a unit of infantry, certain other branches do use the term.

**Corps** – An army formation made up of two or more divisions under the command of a lieutenant general; generally between 30,000 and 60,000 all ranks. Also the collective name for units of a similar type, as in The Royal Canadian Army Service Corps, whose many units provided transportation, catering, and other basic support services to the army.

**Cruiser** – A fast, medium-sized warship with medium armament and armour. Often used as the mainstay of the defence of a convoy or of a patrol to safeguard shipping lanes from enemy surface ships.

**Destroyer** – A warship armed mainly with torpedoes and anti-submarine devices. The small, fast, manoeuvrable workhorse of the navies; it was originally called a "torpedo-boat destroyer."

**Division** – An army formation made up of two or more brigades, usually 15,000 or more men. It is commanded by a major general. The Canadian Army had both infantry and armoured (i.e. tank) divisions.

**Field Marshal** – The highest rank in the British Army. The other services' equivalent ranks are Admiral of the Fleet and Marshal of the Royal Air Force.

**Formation** – The army term for a body of troops larger than a battalion (e.g. brigade, division).

**Group** – A large air force formation, usually composed of four or more squadrons and the bases from which they operated. The largest Canadian group was Number 6 (RCAF) Group of the British Bomber Command. By 1945, Number 6 (RCAF) Group included 14 squadrons that operated nearly 300 heavy four-engine bombers from 10 bases in northern England.

**Non-commissioned Officer (NCO)** – A Commonwealth serviceman holding an army rank from corporal to staff sergeant inclusive (to flight sergeant in the air forces).

**Pillbox** – A small concrete fort constructed on the Normandy beaches by the Germans as part of their anti-invasion fortifications.

**Platoon** – A body of about 30 men, commanded by a subaltern (next rank below captain) officer. There are three or four platoons to a company.

**Slit Trench** – A narrow trench dug for the protection of a small number of people

**Squadron** – The basic unit of the air force, usually 10 to 18 aircraft.

**SS** – Abbreviation of the German Schutzstaffel-Protection Patrol. A Nazi political policing force of evil reputation, gained particularly for their brutal role in extermination camps such as Belsen and Auschwitz. The Waffen (Armed) SS were part of the German armed forces and distinct from the concentration camp guards.

## Appendix B

**Subaltern** – A commissioned army officer below the rank of captain (i.e. a second lieutenant or lieutenant).

**Tank** – An armoured and armed fighting vehicle, driven and steered by its tracks. The word was originally a code word in World War I, used to mislead the enemy over what was about to be secretly supplied to the troops on the front lines.

**Vergeltungswaffen:** V1 and V2 – Translates as "weapons of revenge." V1 was the code name given by the Germans to their jet-propelled, pilotless aircraft with a one-ton warhead. Much used against London from June 1944, it was inaccurate but successful over such a large target area. Also much used against Antwerp, Belgium. Vulnerable to anti-aircraft guns and fighters. V2 was the code name given by the Germans to their large rocket, also with a one-ton warhead. Its speed meant that there was no warning of its arrival and no defence against it.

**Victoria Cross (VC)** – The highest decoration for valour in the Commonwealth forces. It takes precedence over all other orders and decorations, and is equal in merit but senior to the George Cross. The act of valour must be performed in face of the enemy and the VC can be awarded to a person of any rank. The obverse is inscribed simply "FOR VALOUR."

**Wing** – An air force formation made up of two or more squadrons.

# *Appendix C*
# Canadian Weaponry

The following is a list of the main weaponry used by the Canadian troops during World War II.

**Armoured Bulldozer:** The armoured bulldozer was a conventional Caterpiller diesel tractor, fitted with a dozer blade and plated with armour to protect the engine and driver. It carried no armament and often came under heavy fire. On D-Day, this machinery was vital in clearing beach obstacles, unclogging openings in sea walls, and constructing ramps to let tanks and vehicles drive inland off the beach. Armoured bulldozers later proved invaluable for clearing streets of rubble, filling bomb craters, and clearing roadblocks.

**AVRE:** The Armoured Vehicle Royal Engineer (AVRE) was a Churchill tank, mounted with a "Petard" spigot mortar (large-calibre short-range gun) that could throw a 40-pound "dustbin" about 140 metres. The engineers used it to destroy emplacements such as concrete barriers, roadblocks, and pillboxes. In addition to the Petard, the AVRE could also be mounted with an assault bridge, crane, or dozer blade. The "Flail," "Crocodile," and "Ark" (a moving bridge) were related vehicles.

## Appendix C

**Bangalore Torpedo:** The Bangalore Torpedo was a simple explosive device, first used extensively on D-Day by Allied troops to clear barricades, mines, and barbed wire. The torpedo was manually portable and consisted of three different sections: nose sections for penetrating obstacles, explosive sections filled with TNT or C4, and hollow sections of pipe to give the device the required length. Up to four sections, each three inches wide by six feet long, could be connected by metal collars. Deployed by one or two soldiers, the tube was placed on the ground and then pushed forward below bunkers, tank traps, barbed wire entanglements, or by mine fields and then detonated with either a remote-controlled electric detonator or a non-electric blasting cap with delayed-action fuse.

**Bren Machine Gun:** The Bren Gun was a .303 calibre light machine gun with a 30-round magazine. It formed the basis of firepower of the infantry company. The Bren was employed one per infantry section of 10 men (or three per platoon). Each section had a Bren group (four men) led by a lance corporal, one other rifleman, a Bren Gunner (Number One on the Bren), and his assistant (Number Two on the Bren). The Bren was also used as a vehicle-mounted weapon on Universal Carriers (which were often referred to as Bren Gun Carriers due to this armament).

**Colt 1911 .45:** Made in the United States by Colt Arms, the Colt 1911 .45 found its way to England via the Lend-Lease Act, where it quickly became one of the favourite sidearms of

British forces due to its powerful .45 calibre bullet. The Colt 1911 featured a seven-round detachable magazine and a rear grip safety in addition to the standard semi-automatic safety.

**Crab:** The Crab (or Flail) was a Sherman tank with a power-operated flailing attachment that could clear a three-metre wide path through a minefield. The flail was a rotating drum, powered by a drive from the tank engine and held by two girders extending from the front of the tank. Attached to the drum were 43 chains, each with an iron ball. When the drum was rotated the chains beat the ground and exploded mines to a depth of 10 inches. Churchill tanks were also used for Flails.

**Crocodile:** The Crocodile flamethrower tank was a modified Churchill Mark VII with a flamethrower gun mounted in place of the hull machine gun. The flame gun had a range of 110 metres.

**Duplex Drive (DD) Tank:** The DD tanks were Shermans with twin propellers and a collapsible canvas screen with rubber air tubes that provided floatation. The canvas screen was reinforced by struts and secured to a deck around the tank hull. The tank hung suspended underneath the canvas boat, which provided positive buoyancy. The DD was powered by two propellers geared to the engine, and could travel at five knots in the water. It was steered by swivelling the screws. The DD tanks were carried on Landing Craft Tanks (LCTs) to about 6400 metres from shore, where they were launched into the water. The tanks would swim into shore and land

# Appendix C

with the charging infantry. When the tracks grounded on the beach, the canvas sides were collapsed and tanks would be ready to fight. The DD tanks were the solution to providing immediate armoured support for the assault troops on D-Day. These Shermans were armed with a 75mm gun and two .30 calibre Browning machine guns.

**5.5-Inch Gun / Howitzer:** The 5.5-inch gun/howitzer was used by the Canadians as a medium artillery weapon. It fired an 82-pound high-explosive projectile up to 16,500 metres at two rounds a minute. It was operated by a ten-man crew and was towed by a five-ton tractor known as a Matador.

**The Funnies:** The assault on Juno Beach used armoured vehicles known as "Funnies," devised by Sir Percy Hobart. To many, these vehicles were the difference between success and failure. The British 79th Armoured Division and the Royal Engineers had been given the task of delivering a variety of special armoured vehicles (AVREs) that could perform battlefield engineering tasks including clearing minefields, dropping fascines (long bundles of sticks bound together, used in building earthworks) into anti-tank ditches, and laying bridges. Armoured regiments were equipped with DD (duplex drive) Sherman tanks which could "swim" in the water and then travel on land to support the leading waves of infantry.

**Grenades:** The grenade, a small, simple bomb, was used with great effect by the infantry in assaults on pillboxes, machine-gun nests, and small groups of soldiers. Once the safety pin is pulled, a striker lever is held in place by the soldier's grip until the grenade is thrown. When the lever is released, a striker ignites a fuse; there is a delay of four to five seconds as the grenade travels to its target and explodes into shrapnel pieces. The Type 36 grenade could be either thrown or fired from a rifle and was widely used by Canadian troops. Other grenade types included the No. 74 anti-tank grenade and phosphorous grenade.

**Half-Track:** A half-track is a vehicle that utilizes both tracks and wheels as running gear. The half-track was conceived by the Russians around 1914, but was successfully developed by the Citroen Company in France.

**Inglis Mk I Browning:** The Inglis Mk I Browning was a 9mm semi-automatic pistol with a 13-round magazine. The Inglis Browning was a copy of the Browning Hi-Power, designed by John Browning and manufactured in Belgium. The model was built in Canada by Inglis of Canada for all British forces, from February 1944 until September 1945. Many British and Commonwealth soldiers carried either the Browning or the Colt 1911 for its rapid-fire capabilities and stopping power. It was carried by officers, NCOs, and specialist ranks only.

**Landing Craft:** The amphibious assault called for extensive use of specialized landing craft, including LCIs, LCTs, and LCAs, to carry the infantry, vehicles, and equipment to the beaches.

    **LCA** – Landing Craft, Assault
    **LCG** – Landing craft, Gun

## Appendix C

**LCI** - Landing Craft, Infantry
**LCM** - Landing Craft, Mechanized
**LCP** - Landing Craft, Personnel
**LCS** - Landing Craft, Support
**LCT** - Landing Craft, Tank
**LCT®** - Landing Craft, Tank (Rocket)
**LCVP** - Landing Craft, Vehicle and Personnel
**LSH** - Landing Ship, Headquarters
**LSI** - Landing Ship, Infantry
**LST** - Landing Ship, Tank

**Lee Enfield Rifle, No. 4, Mark I:** The Canadian infantry used the Lee Enfield rifle as their standard weapon throughout World War II. The Short Magazine Lee Enfield No.1 was used up until November 1942, when the No. 4 was issued. In June 1943, the Canadians started using the No. 4 model made in Canada (designated the Mark I). Its box-type magazine, extending through the bottom of the stock forward of the trigger guard, carried two five-round clips of .303 ammunition. The Lee Enfield was the fastest operating bolt-action rifle in the world. A trained soldier could fire 10 rounds per minute and be effective up to 820 metres, although ranges up to 550 metres were more common. Various sights could be fitted, and it could also launch a grenade from a cup adapter or discharger. A superior locking system and easy field maintenance made the Lee Enfield superior to most other bolt-action rifles. Canada manufactured almost a million Lee Enfields during the war.

**PIAT (Projector Infantry, Anti-Tank):** The 32-pound PIAT was a cross between an anti-tank rifle and a bazooka. It fired a 2.5-pound anti-tank grenade up to 90 metres. The PIAT was effective against all German tanks if fired accurately at the side armour. It was simple in design, construction, and operation, but it had considerable recoil. A bomb was slid onto a spigot inside the launcher, and when the trigger was pulled, the spigot struck and detonated the bomb's propellant cartridge, firing the bomb.

**The Priest:** The Priest was a self-propelled gun used by the Canadian artillery regiments. The 105mm howitzer fired a 33-pound high explosive shell up to 10,400 metres and could also be used against tanks. It had a crew of seven and could travel up to 38 kilometres per hour. The Americans called it the "Gun Motor Carriage 105mm howitzer M7" but the British nicknamed it the Priest because of the pulpit-like machine gun mounting.

**Sherman:** The Sherman tank was the workhorse of the Canadian Armoured Corps during the Second World War. The most widely used version was the M4A4 (Sherman V). The Sherman had a crew of five: commander, gunner, loader-operator, driver and co-driver. The 30-ton Sherman had a speed of 38 kilometres per hour and a range of 160 kilometres. It was armed with a 75mm gun and two .30 calibre Browning machine guns. The armour was two inches thick on the hull front, 1.5 inches on the sides, three inches on the front turret, and two inches on the turret sides. It was powered by a 30 cylinder Chrysler multi-bank gasoline engine (five 6-cylinder engines) and was very reliable. The Shermans were outgunned by the German tanks, but very fast and manoeuvrable. Discarded tracks and sandbags were often added to give extra frontal protection. Some Shermans, known as Fireflies, were mounted with a 17-pounder gun. The regiments of the 2nd Armoured Brigade were provided with about a dozen Fireflies each, just prior to D-Day, for increased firepower against the more heavily armoured German tanks.

**6-Pounder Anti-Tank Gun:** The 6-pounder was the main anti-tank gun of the Canadian infantry units and anti-tank regiments after 1942. Its effective range was 900 metres. It was usually towed by a Universal Carrier, and was largely replaced by the 17-pounder anti-tank gun in 1944.

**Staghound Armoured Car:** The Staghound Armoured Car was used by reconnaissance regiments for patrols to get intelligence, conduct raids, protect convoys, and guard head-quarters. It had a crew of five, could travel up to 90 kilometres per hour, and had a range of 800 kilometres. It was armed with a 37mm gun and two .30 machine guns.

**Sten Gun:** The Sten Gun was a 9mm submachine gun with a 32-round detachable magazine box. First used by Canadian troops at Dieppe, it had completely replaced the Thompson submachine gun by the time of the Normandy landings. The Mark I Sten, which featured a flash hider, wooden furniture, and folding handgrip, was quickly replaced by the Sten Mark

II. Two million Mark IIs were produced and saw widespread use. The Sten was a simply built weapon, manufactured from just 47 parts, mainly stamped from steel and welded, sweated, pressed, or riveted together. The only machined parts were the bolt and barrel. The Sten was issued to vehicle crews, despatch riders, and those who had no need for a long-range weapon. It was also issued to infantry battalions, especially platoon commanders, platoon sergeants, and section leaders in infantry platoons.

**3-Inch Mortar:** The 3-inch mortar was the standard heavy mortar used by the infantry battalions support company to provide extra firepower. It could lob shells into enemy positions from a high angle, and could hit targets from as close as 110 metres to a maximum of 2500 metres. A crew of three transported it in a Universal Carrier and handled it as three separate parts: the smooth bore barrel, the base plate, and the mounting, which supported the barrel by providing elevating and transversing adjustments. Once set up, a 10-pound bomb was dropped down the barrel to hit a striker stud, which fired a propellant cartridge in the tail of the bomb. When the bomb landed, a striker in the bomb set off its explosive. Three types of mortar bombs were used: smoke, high explosive, and star. There was also a 4.2-inch mortar that fired a 20-pound bomb. The infantry platoons also used a 2-inch mortar that fired a 2.5-pound bomb.

**25-Pounder Gun / Howitzer:** The 25-pounder was the main gun used by the Commonwealth field artillery. It could be used as a gun, for firing armour-piercing shells at a flat trajectory, or as a howitzer firing high explosive shells at a high angle. It was effective up to 11,300 metres, and up to 12,000 with a supercharge. When in use, the gun was usually mounted on a circular firing platform, which, by moving the trail, permitted a 360° traverse. The traverse of the gun when used without the firing platform was limited to 8° and its elevation to 45°. It was operated by a six-man crew. Canada manufactured the 25-pounder starting in July 1941.

**Universal Carrier:** The Universal Carrier (or Bren carrier) was a lightly armoured tracked vehicle that could travel up to 55 kilometres per hour and carry four to six soldiers and their weapons. The men had protection against small arms fire but no overhead protection. The Universal Carrier had many uses: reconnaissance, the transporting of troops, wounded men, food, mortars, or machine guns, the towing of anti-tank guns, and as a headquarters vehicle. When used as a weapons carrier, it was fitted with Vickers .303 machine guns, Bren light machine guns, or 2-inch mortars.

**Vickers .303 Machine Gun:** Canadians used the Vickers .303 machine gun during both world wars. Classed as a medium weapon, the Vickers gun could be fired at high or low angles from a tripod. It operated on a simple gas-assisted recoil system and was water-cooled. The Vickers was fed by 250 round cloth belts of .303 ammunition and fired in full automatic bursts of 10 to 20 rounds. It could fire 60 shots per minute (rated as slow fire) and 250 shots per minute as rapid fire.

It was accurate up to 1000 metres but could reach much farther. A soldier fired the weapon by grasping both traversing handles and depressing the trigger with both thumbs. The gun fired fully automatically as long as the trigger was depressed and until it ran out of ammunition.

# Bibliography

Botting, Douglas. *The D-Day Invasion.* New York: Time-Life Books Inc., 1978.

Bruce, George. *Second Front Now.* London: Macdonald and Jane's Publishers, 1979.

Granatstein, J.L. and Desmond Morton. *A Nation Forged In Fire.* Toronto: Lester & Orpen Dennys, 1989.

Granatstein, J. L. and Desmond Morton. *Bloody Victory.* Toronto: Lester Publishing Limited, 1994.

Granatstein, J. L. *Normandy 1944-1999.* Ottawa: Minister of Supply & Services, 1999.

Haswell, Jock. *The Intelligence and Deception of the D-Day Landings.* London: BT Batsford Ltd., 1979.

Hesketh, Roger. *Fortitude: The D-Day Deception Campaign.* London: St. Ermin's Press, 1999.

Johnson, Johnnie. *Wing Leader.* New York: Ballantine Books, 1957.

McKee, Alexander. *Caen: Anvil of Victory.* London: Souvenir Press Ltd., 2000.

Munro, Ross. *Gauntlet to Overlord.* Toronto: The Macmillan Co. of Canada Limited, 1945.

Peart, Hugh and John Schaffer. *The Winds of Change.* Toronto: Ryerson Press, 1961.

Reader's Digest Association Ltd. *The Canadians at War: Volumes 1&2.* Montreal, 1969.

Wilmot, Chester. *The Struggle for Europe.* Westport, Ct.: Greenwood Publishing Group, 1972.

Windrow, Martin. *The Soldier's Story: D-Day and the Battle of Normandy.* London: Compendium Publishing Ltd., 2001.

# Acknowledgements

The author relied heavily on the two-volume Reader's Digest account of *The Canadians at War* for much of the information related in this book. Another source that proved a wealth of information was the Veterans Affairs Canada booklet "Normandy 1944-1999," issued to commemorate the 55th anniversary of D-Day and written by J.L. Granatstein, the dean of Canadian military history. Two other Granatstein books, co-authored with Desmond Morton, were also very helpful, as was Ross Munro's *Gauntlet to Overlord.* There were many other books, magazines, newspaper clippings, and web sites that helped fill in the gaps. Two web sites worth noting are Johnny Canuck's Wartime History of Canada (www.nt.net/~toby/) and The Loyal Edmonton Regiment Museum (www.lermuseum.org).

But the most important source was the many veterans the author has spoken with over the years. Primary amongst these was his late father, Sergeant H.M. (Mel) Douglas, affectionately known as "Daddy Warbooks" for all the post-war WWII reading he did.

Thanks also go to good friend Janet Short who, as a young girl living in the vicinity of Chartwell during World War II, actually befriended The Great Statesman, Sir Winston

Churchill. She has been a wealth of information, advice, and encouragement.

# Photo Credits

All photos from National Archives of Canada: PA 137013 (front cover), PA 129053 (pg.39), PA 129056 (pg. 55), PA 33966 (pg. 64), PA 171084 (pg. 71), PA 131404 (pg. 92)

# About The Author

Tom Douglas is the author of another book of military history in the *Amazing Stories* series — *Canadian Spies*. His father, the late H.M. (Mel) Douglas, was a veteran who served with the 19th Field Regiment and was part of the D-Day invasion.

As an elementary school teacher, Tom served with DND Schools Overseas in Metz, France. During that posting, he visited numerous Canada battle sites and cemeteries in Europe. He left teaching to become a reporter with *The Sault Ste. Marie Star*, and has worked in communications ever

since. As a reporter, he was selected by DND to tour Canadian bases in Europe on two occasions.

After working with Canadian Press, and serving as publisher/owner of a weekly newspaper in Queensland, Australia, Tom was hired as communications consultant to The Honourable Bennett Campbell, Minister of Veterans Affairs, in Ottawa.

He travelled with the minister and groups of World War I, World War II, and Korean veterans on pilgrimages involving Vimy Ridge, Normandy, Brittany, Rome, and Seoul. He was also part of a Canadian delegation that was invited by French President Francois Mitterrand to attend Remembrance Day services at the Arch of Triumph.

Tom accompanied Veterans Affairs Minister Campbell to Europe for the 40th anniversary of D-Day in 1984. They took two side trips — one to unveil a plaque in Rome in honour of the Canada/U.S. Special Services force that liberated the Eternal City, the other to Brittany to honour French-Canadian soldiers who had parachuted into Occupied France to set up an escape network for Allied personnel. This latter experience was the inspiration for the *Canadian Spies* book.

Tom and his wife, also a published author with the *Amazing Stories* line, organized a special 50th anniversary D-Day voyage to Normandy on the *Queen Elizabeth 2* in 1994. The ship was entirely taken over by D-Day veterans, their relatives, and military historians, who were entertained

onboard by Bob Hope, Vera Lynn, and the Glenn Miller Orchestra.

The following year, Tom led a group of Canadian veterans and their relatives on a five-country bus tour of Europe as part of the commemoration of the 50th anniversary of the Allied Victory in Europe (VE Day).

More recently, Tom has written speeches for senior officials of DND and Veterans Affairs Canada. He has also interviewed veterans as the basis for several news articles that have been distributed on the Veterans Affairs' web site and to newspapers across Canada. He currently serves as copy editor of *The Canadian Military Journal*, and is a member of The Memory Project, speaking to schoolchildren about the meaning of Remembrance Day.

Tom is a member of Branch 114, Royal Canadian Legion.